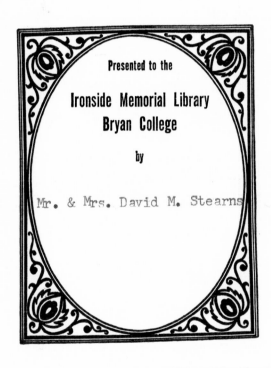

WHITE AND BLACK: *Test of a Nation*

Books by Samuel Lubell

WHITE AND BLACK: TEST OF A NATION

REVOLT OF THE MODERATES

REVOLUTION IN WORLD TRADE

THE FUTURE OF AMERICAN POLITICS

WHITE AND BLACK:

Test of a Nation

Second Edition, Revised

Samuel Lubell

Harper Colophon Books
Harper & Row, Publishers
New York

Dedicated to the memory of MARTIN SOMMERS *who pushed me into political writing*

WHITE AND BLACK: TEST OF A NATION. *Copyright © 1964, 1966 by Samuel Lubell. Printed in the United States of America. All rights reserved. No part of this book may be used or reproduced in any manner whatsoever without written permission except in the case of brief quotations embodied in critical articles and reviews. For information address Harper & Row, Publishers, Incorporated, 49 East 33rd Street, New York, N.Y., 10016.*

First HARPER COLOPHON *edition published 1966 by Harper & Row, Publishers, Incorporated, New York*

Library of Congress Catalog Card Number: 66-2793

Contents

v

Preface to the Second Edition

Every critical problem contains a hidden fourth dimension that is too often overlooked — the dimension of time.

With our raging racial crisis, this remains by far the most important of all dimensions. Whatever the explosive event — whether it happens in Mississippi or in the Watts district of Los Angeles — the triggering incident is but the fuse for a bomb made of past neglects, of neglects that still live, work, sulk and agitate inside of many Negroes.

And even while we struggle to cut into the effects of time that is past, new neglects in the South and in Northern slums continue to be burdened onto the time that will be the future.

In *White and Black* I have tried to explore this dimension of racial time; also to report the changes in American thinking and feeling as we struggle to catch up with time.

Two developments since the writing of the first edition make the future more hopeful. First, it is steadily becoming clearer that no magic overnight "solution" to our racial troubles is possible. With this realization, we are gaining a more realistic appreciation of what remains to be done. The mere passage of civil rights legislation, we have learned, settles nothing.

Second, the preponderant majority of Americans have demonstrated a strong desire to find some way of uniting the nation in racial peace.

This desire, shared by most, though by no means all of the people, was evidenced in the crushing defeat suffered by Senator Barry Goldwater. Because of its importance, I have added to this second edition of *White and Black* a fairly full account of the racial aspects of Johnson's 1964 sweep. Goldwater's sole hope for victory hinged on being able to unite the backlash of anti-Negro resentment in the North with the racial angers of the white South. For two tingling months it seemed that this effort had a chance of succeeding, but in the end, the yearning for racial peace emerged triumphant to swell Johnson's majority.

In this revised edition I have also sought to define more sharply what it means to live with a continuing racial crisis that cannot be resolved for some time to come no matter what is done today. This harsh fact argues for a new emphasis on the *quality* of racial action. Between action and inaction our choice must continue to be action; but simply "doing something" needs to be replaced by doing what is effective.

SAMUEL LUBELL

November, 1965

Acknowledgments

The first thought of writing this book was inspired by an invitation to deliver the Sidney Hillman lectures at Howard University early in 1957. Competing projects led me to drop the idea, but it was rekindled when the Institute of Industrial Relations at UCLA had me give another series of lectures in 1961 on the main forces reshaping American politics.

Still it remained for the Birmingham demonstrations to provide the final impetus to dig out of my files the notes that had been accumulating and to complete this book.

The fact that this book has been in the thinking for so long makes it difficult to recall all of the many persons who have helped me. Most of the research for this volume was done by Bruce Stave, a highly perceptive graduate student now at the University of Pittsburgh. Stave made available to me material he has collected for his doctoral dissertation on the New Deal's impact on the urban political machine.

Others who helped in research and interviewing were Esther Kartiganer, now with CBS, and Dale Burman, now at Principia College.

The manuscript was improved immeasurably by the editing aid of Walter Everett of the American Press Institute.

Valuable suggestions came from Morris B. Abram, Leslie Dunbar of the Southern Regional Council, and his predecessor, Harold Fleming, also George Goodwin of the First National Bank of Atlanta, Ga.; Christopher F. Edley and Paul Ylvisaker of the Ford Foundation.

Professor Eli Ginzburg of Columbia University and Herman Miller of the U.S. Census Bureau were particularly helpful in discussing the changing economic status of the Negro. Calvin Beale of the U.S. Department of Agriculture supplied data on how rapidly the Negro has been losing out in Southern agriculture. These figures have not been used in the study, but they gave me a basis for judgment of these trends.

Herbert Hill of the NAACP was consulted on Negro labor developments; Henry Lee Moon, also of the NAACP, as usual helped guide me to various sources of information. The Field Foundation kindly let me read in manuscript a study on the Student Protest Movement in the South.

For assistance in collecting voting returns and information on school and other conditions in specific communities I am indebted to many persons including: Barbara Stanton and Frank Angelo of the Detroit *Free Press;* J. William Jones of the Philadelphia *Bulletin;* George Killenberg and Bob Jackson of the St. Louis *Globe-Democrat;* Dean Schoel-kopf and John Stanton of the Chicago *Daily News;* Leo Baron and Dick Thornburg of the Cincinnati *Post and Times-Star;* Brady Black of the Cincinnati *Enquirer;* Ben Hite, Los Angeles County Registrar of Voters; Elmer Bertelson of the Houston *Chronicle;* and Clark Porteous of the Memphis *Press-Scimitar.*

Finally, this book adds another heaping of appreciation for my wife, Helen Sopot Lubell, who, as in the past, served as Lady Pooh-Bah, doing something of everything that had to be done to get this manuscript out.

Foreword

In the spring of 1961, a few months after John F. Kennedy took office as President of the United States, the Institute of Industrial Relations of the University of California, Los Angeles, presented a series of public lectures under the title *Reshaping American Politics: Labor and the Kennedy Administration*. The three lectures were entitled: "Did Kennedy Restore the New Deal Coalition?"; "Labor, the Negro and the South"; and "Labor in a Managed Economy."

In his second lecture Mr. Lubell, while analyzing the politics of the civil rights issue, voiced the judgment that Negro strategy in the immediate years ahead would try to force a racial showdown that would compel the President to intervene decisively on behalf of speeded integration. The years since 1961 have witnessed the validation of this analysis.

In *White and Black* Samuel Lubell has expanded and updated his UCLA lectures to present his appraisal of what the "Negro Revolution" portends for America's future. His is not an optimistic view, warning as he does that "we may be destroying our capacity ever to resolve our racial difficulties" and that we are being "ripped into two separate nations with segregated skins."

In this study of our racial crisis, Mr. Lubell demonstrates anew the qualities which have gained him such distinction as a student of American political behavior. He is a journalist who has won a reputation for predicting election results and for analyzing changing political trends for newspapers, magazines and over radio and television. He also has a historian's sensitivity to the workings of time and change as shown in *The Future of American Politics* written more than a decade ago.

The Institute of Industrial Relations at UCLA is pleased to have had the opportunity to provide the forum for the lectures from which this book was to emerge.

BENJAMIN AARON, DIRECTOR
Institute of Industrial Relations
University of California, Los Angeles

1

Racial Showdown

"Freedom Now!"

This is a study of time, public opinion and America's most tragic problem.

It is an exploration of how the American people — white and black — have used the hundred years between two presidential assassinations in dealing with the racial conflict which threatens to tear apart our society, as it did in 1860.

The evidence uncovered points to striking advances but it also warns that as a nation we are in danger of losing control of the problem. Unless the thinking of both whites and Negroes is changed we may destroy our capacity ever to resolve our racial difficulties.

Half of the war has been won. Since reconstruction, the South had resisted any national racial policy, fighting always for a free hand to deal with the Negro as a "peculiar" Southern problem. In voting against the Civil Rights Law of 1964, Barry Goldwater transformed the election into a referendum

1

on separatism against unity as our goal. The decisiveness with which Goldwater was defeated, his failure even to carry with him more than half of the South, means that the century-long battle to establish a *national* racial policy is over.

A historic turning point!

But our commitment, at long last, to a national racial policy does not make it certain that we will become a unified nation racially. The testing, testing, testing of our habits and our minds will go on, more intensely perhaps than in the past.

Whether we win — or lose — this second half of the war will hinge largely on our understanding of why this racial crisis whirled up on us as it did, how far it has taken us and what more remains to be done; also on how the nature of the crisis changes even as we, the people, change our thinking and feeling.

In its first stage the "Negro Revolution" was largely a struggle to shock us out of indifference and into commitment. The more militant Negro leadership has been bent upon transforming the entire country into one national arena of racial conflict. By stirring tensions at enough points of society, these militants have been determined to involve each of us ever more deeply in their grievances, to leave us no escape from their clamors for "freedom now," no place to hide from taking sides. Among white people the shock of this confrontation touched off divided emotions.

When the Birmingham demonstrations broke loose late in the spring of 1963 I was traveling through the country on an interviewing survey. The photographs of Negroes being toppled by water hoses or fleeing before police dogs shocked most people. Still, many persons tried at first to treat it as primarily a Southern affair.

But as sit-ins, lie-ins, stand-ins and other picketings erupted through the Northern cities, often into one's own community, the temper of public feeling changed. There was a surge of fear.

"I was walking in Harlem," recalled one newspaperman's wife. "Suddenly I realized mine was the only white face on the streets! I had to get out of there. You could sense the revenge they wanted to take out on the white man."

A Cleveland salesman confessed, "I never thought they would rise up this way. They deserve these rights."

Others, including persons who had always considered themselves advocates of Negro advance, were dismayed by Negro demands for a specific percentage of jobs or that white children should be bussed into Negro schools. A frequently voiced grumble ran "White people have rights too."

Almost everyone sensed that the basic nature of the civil rights struggle had changed abruptly. It was like being on a ship which without warning veers off course into a storm, with the passengers and crew demanding, "What's got into the captain? Where is he taking us?"

Basically, I believe, we are being rushed along by two sets of forces. First, the postwar years have churned up social and economic changes which compelled the Negro to redefine his standing in American society. Second, in struggling to do so the Negro found himself forced to revolt against the prevailing pattern of racial bargaining.

One target of Negro impatience was the tactic of endless

Southern litigation. In its 1954 ruling the Supreme Court
sought to give the South time to adjust to gradual desegregation of schools. But many Southern states seized upon the
phrase "with due deliberate speed" as a pretext to do little
or nothing until forced by the Court. Case after case was
dragged out as if each involved a new issue. On the eve of
the Birmingham demonstrations less than half of one percent
of the Negro children in the eleven secession states were
attending integrated schools — this after nearly nine years
of court action.

The second bargaining trap from which the Negroes have
been trying to spring free is that rigged by our political
parties. The prevailing stratagem was to play off the Northern Negro and the white Southerner against one another so
as to yield the Negro some gains but never as much as
promised nor too much at one time.

Of course, there is much to be said for employing our
party system to postpone or avoid painful, nation-splitting
decisions. A small library of books has been written around
the theme that the distinctive genius of the American system
of political coalition lies in the compulsions it exerts upon
extremists to moderate their demands in order to gain
general support.

But for moderation and compromise to prove wise one
requirement is indispensable—the time gained must operate
to bring into existence the conditions that will alleviate and
reconcile the antagonisms that are so difficult to resolve.
If the workings of time aggravate the problem, then our
party system is failing the nation.

This is the crucial, agonizing question at the heart of our

raging racial conflict: Is time, as we are using it, bringing into being conditions that eventually will enable us to overcome our differences or is time eroding our ability *ever* to resolve this conflict?

Perhaps the most heartening sign is the fact that the Negro has been able to fight so vigorously for his rights — something he could not do as late as a generation ago. Nor should so much agitation dismay us. Conflict has always served the United States as the furnace that melts away the divisive impurities of the past to produce new, stronger alloys of unity.

But if this strife is to unify and not divide us a more strenuous and disciplined effort will be needed than most of us have yet contemplated. Widely held illusions that tend to deceive us into believing lesser exertions are adequate need to be dumped. Five in particular:

1. That the workings of progress are *automatic* and that Negroes are *bound* to better their status with time.

2. That economic improvement will solve our racial crisis.

3. That voting power is the weapon that eventually will bring the Negro victory in his struggle.

4. That racial resistance in the South is the "last gasp of a dying social order," which is being killed off by industrialization and urbanization.

5. That Negroes can be absorbed into our society in much the same way as other minority and one-time immigrant groups have been in the past.

Some of these illusions spring from our congenital national optimism. Americans have always taken for granted the inevitability of progress, possibly because nearly all our favorite yardsticks—from land values to the stock market— keep hitting new highs. But our history shows that Negroes bear a peculiarly harsh vulnerability which forces them to fight anew to hold their place in society whenever drastic social and economic changes occur.

The nature of the struggle has also left us with a fragmented focus, on bits and pieces rather than the whole. Progress in civil rights has never been won evenly, across the line. Instead the pattern has been a thrust here and there, a breakthrough for one effort, a repulse for another.

Setbacks at one point spur a more vigorous assault at some other. As a result, school administrators find themselves under compulsion to remedy evils generated by residential segregation. In migrating north the Southern Negro brings with him neglects he has suffered since childhood. Enormous energies are expended in gaining the Negro the right to vote, partly because it happens to be the right which meets with the least white resistance. Yet voting is a particularly slow hatching egg of power.

The "coming of age" of every other minority group in this country has demonstrated that political effectiveness reflects not votes alone but all the economic resources and intellectual abilities the group can command. No *one* means of advance can be pushed far ahead of the whole front.

Political warfare is also the carrier of its own special trickery. So much of politics consists of marching symbols up the hill and then marching them down again that one always runs the risk of winning psychological battles which bring little real change in the handicaps that Negroes live under.

Perhaps it is foolhardy to attempt to fit the scattered parts of this struggle into a unified whole. Certainly some of my judgments and findings will be challenged. Factors of importance have undoubtedly been overlooked or underestimated. Still the effort seemed worth making, if only to provide the reader with a basis for organizing his own thoughts in disagreement.

One Nation or Two

In essence the shock vibrations rocking our society are the none too rhythmic interactions between two racial confilicts—that in the South and that in the North and West.

The contagion of Negro militancy has swept up out of the South. There the arena of conflict is largely a rural-urban one. The old order is indeed being killed off by new urbanizing forces—at varying mortality rates in different states. But consciously and subconsciously the effort is being made to transfer the racial attitudes of the rural past to the newer urban South. Still, as one new ferment, in some Southern cities Negroes have developed enough of a middle class to fight for a new status for themselves.

In the North and on the Pacific Coast the struggle is not as sharply defined but can perhaps be visualized best as a conflict of the central cities versus the suburbs. The one influence most disruptive of race relations has been the continued flow of Southern Negroes into the larger Northern

cities. Since World War I nearly 5 million Negroes have
moved north, nearly one third of them in the 1950-1960
decade alone. This migration, coupled with the flight of
white families to the suburbs, is overwhelming our larger
cities, reducing them to hopelessly inadequate political units
for their burden of problems.

At the same time jobs have been moving out of the older
industrial states, which have traditionally drawn the heaviest
Negro migrations. The jobs left are walled in by labor
unions and other economic rigidities. While older Negroes
fight against being pushed out of the job citadel, younger
ones batter at the walls for admission.

By the fall of 1963 the tensions generated by these
Southern and Northern racial conflicts threatened to tear
apart the Democratic party. In six weeks of interviewing
through twenty states I found almost the whole South
seething in political anger against President John F. Kennedy. In many Northern states as well, a bitter backlash
had developed among white Democrats against Negro demonstrations and demands. Cities like Philadelphia, Chicago,
Cleveland and Detroit showed heavy enough defections
among ordinarily Democratic voters to have imperiled Kennedy's chances of being re-elected.

After Kennedy's assassination I went out again, revisiting
some of the neighborhoods I had been in a few weeks earlier.
The tragedy at Dallas had been such a shock to the regional
manager of one Philadelphia insurance company that for the
first time he had hired a Negro claims adjuster. "I don't
know how it will work," said this insurance manager, "but
I felt it was the right thing to do."

Generally throughout the nation the desire was strong to patch together some easing of racial tensions. Only a month earlier the voters I had talked with had voiced their angers as if they were building up to a showdown fight. After Kennedy's death most people talked as if they wanted to climb down out of that fight.

In his bid for the presidency, Goldwater sought to merge Southern angers with the backlash discontents among Northern whites. Why he failed so badly is explained in detail in later chapters. Basically, though, Goldwater failed because the politics of race in the South did not meet the needs of the rest of the nation. In the South the dominant drive has been to keep the Negroes and whites as separate as possible. In the North and West the need has been for a politics which would enable whites and Negroes to live together.

That so many Americans, who protested "Negroes are pushing too far," still voted against Goldwater is striking evidence of how strong was the popular desire to unify rather than divide the nation racially, to lessen, not intensify, the raging conflict, to heal, not inflame.

Still, racial peace is not something that can be wished into existence. In fact, for the deadline years immediately ahead, we can be sure that our dilemma will be sharpened, not eased.

"To the white man," one Negro wisely observed, "the solution of the racial crisis means the absence of tension. To me it is getting my rights."

For a full generation and probably longer there will be no facile formula for bridging these two definitions of "solution."

The first harsh, unyielding fact we face is that no solution to our racial crisis is possible today. Given the structure of our society and our minds there is no possible way for Negroes and whites to strike a true racial peace.

The utmost we can do, RIGHT NOW, is to bring into being the conditions of living and thinking which may enable us to achieve racial unity some years from now; how many years is not even in sight.

It is not easy to live with a continuing crisis that cannot be resolved no matter what is done. One is reminded of those Hollywood spectaculars of a storm at sea in which all the ballast and furnishings have broken loose from their ropes and roll and smash with each lurch of the ship.

We must expect the continuing racial crisis to roll and smash blindly. Many Negroes will join James Baldwin in crying "white hypocrisy" no matter what is done. Some whites will shriek "quiet, quiet!" whatever the price.

Still other whites will try to turn this racial crisis into a calculated assault upon the whole of American society.

The Negro cannot be free, we will be told, until capitalism is destroyed, war is abolished and all of us share a "moral catharsis" as color-blinding as Paul experienced at Tarsus. For these assorted pickets of Armageddon — pacifists, communists, socialists, cybernetics, triple revolutionists and sundry other activists — turmoil and disorder may seem the essential precondition for remaking the world.

What will really be at stake in the years ahead is how we use the time of conflict still left to us.

The fundamental choice we now face was expressed rather well by Buel G. Gallagher, who once headed Talladega College for Negroes in Alabama and now is president of City College in New York. In his address before the 1965 convention of the National Association for the Advancement of

Colored People, Gallagher saw the elimination of segregation and other forms of discrimination "in every part of the nation" as "clearly inevitable."

"The question," he posed, "is by what means it is to be accomplished and what the after-results are to be.

"We can pursue our revolutionary goals in such a manner as to leave upon the nation and the world deep and angry scars which do not heal with time, but fester and irritate. Or we can carry the revolution to its conclusion in such a manner as to bring a new unity or serenity to a troubled and divided people. This is the choice to be made . . . in this generation."

It will be an agonizingly difficult choice if only because we must think not only of the speed but of the quality of racial change being sought. In liquidating what is left of the structure of segregation in the South the faster we move the better — at least that is how I read the lesson of what has happened there since 1954.

But the goal that comes after — for whites and Negroes to learn to live together — will be far more treacherous to pursue. Broad principles of justice and brotherhood, on which we may all agree, will have to be given a street-corner reality over which we will disagree sharply.

In the problems that must be dealt with, we will need to learn to separate what is racial from what is non-racial; how much of the sickness of the Northern ghettoes is properly attributed to the failure of Northern society and how much of it reflects the continued influx of Negroes from the South; what can be changed tomorrow and what will have to wait for another dawn.

These efforts to take apart our racial problems will be fought by some Negro leaders who, in their hunger to destroy "the old Magnolia Myth" of Negro inferiority, now strive to blame everything — poverty, murder, rape — on race. Other Negro leaders, in their eagerness to push their bargaining to the limit of the white man's resistance, are inclined to brush aside any facts which indicate some advance is being made.

In the spring of 1965 I attended a conference at which two civil rights leaders talked of Negro unemployment. One contended "The Negro is worse off now than ever"; the other sought to explain it by declaring, "Each year we see a loss of half a million blue-collar jobs, the kind of work which most Negroes are hired for."

That statement would have held true for the years between 1957 and 1961, when the number of manufacturing jobs dropped by 1.8 million. Between 1962 and 1965, though, blue-collar employment jumped by 2.8 million—an increase, not a loss, of more than half a million such jobs each year.

Unemployment still afflicts too many Negroes. However, that so large a job increase can be ignored does point to the need of the importance of more factual thinking about civil rights. Unless we can measure what progress — how much or how little — is being made, we cannot determine what works and what doesn't work; which difficulties have changed and which have not.

The greater the progress that is made, the more important it will become to be able to determine why some Negroes succeed and others fail. All of us — white and black — share a burden of human bondage that we cannot shake off.

The longer the strides made by the Negro, the sharper will become the conflict between his clamorings for "freedom now" and the fact that no human being, of any color, can be completely free, particularly in our own highly structured society.

American history is also world history and our domestic conflicts usually have been part of far-flung upheavals. It is not mere chance that our "Negro Revolution" should spill over onto our streets at the same time that Africa drums with newly created black governments and the rise of Red China stirs the dread of future racial war.

During the years to come, in short, our unresolved racial crisis will batter against all our social and political institutions; against our personal characters and values, our habits of thinking and living. This testing will be made more critical because it will be conducted against a backdrop of world-wide racial conflict.

In one sense this kind of testing is not new for us. An ever-recurring theme in the drama of American politics has been the struggle to form that "more perfect union." Usually in the past the nationalizing forces that were knitting us into a new unity have won out.

For some years now the Negro has been serving as one of the more powerful pressures nationalizing the basis of American politics. What is still not clear is whether he will prove a unifying or disruptive influence, whether this testing will make us one nation again or leave us ripped into two nations with segregated skins.

My own thoughts on what needs to be done to overcome the forces of disunity are contained in the final chapter. These suggestions will displease many civil rights partisans; still they are put forward as projections of what I have learned from my study of our racial crisis.

Every trend of change is history in motion, the past running ahead of us. To be able to guide racial change so it unifies, not divides, we need to identify the important forces rocking our society, to trace them back into the past and see how they shaped the present, then to project these forces as far into the future as our imaginations can carry us, whether we like or dislike where they are taking us. Having done that, we can perhaps position ourselves so as to direct and even alter these forces before they sweep past us.

That is what this book attempts. Part history and part present, it might be described as an experiment in reporting change. For a better understanding of the present I have relied largely on my interviews with Americans of every description during recent years. In the North through these interviews I have sought to probe the divided emotions that most people share and how these inner conflicts propel us to act as we do.

In the South, through eight separate surveys, none more than two years apart, I have followed the fascinating war of public opinion that has been raging since 1954 — the slow, grudging acceptance by white Southerners of token integration, paced by a rising Negro revolt against gradualism. As will be seen, it was President Kennedy's political fate to be caught in the middle when these two trends collided.

But our racial feelings are also the product of our separate histories — the white man's and the black man's. Much of this part of the story is told in terms of the changing patterns of Negro leadership, from Booker T. Washington to Martin Luther King, Jr. Why did each man's aspirations take the form that they did? What led to accomplishment? What bogged them down into frustration?

Each of these leaders is portrayed against the backdrop of the social, economic and political arena in which their fighting was done. This seemed a fair way of appraising their careers and significance.

It has been my belief that the Founding Fathers designed our democracy so that it would indeed constitute an arena in which "we the people" could battle out our contesting interests. Changes in the nature of the American arena constitute, I believe, the most valid measure we have for evaluating American democracy.

Our narrative therefore begins with the man who was the recognized leader of the Negroes when they were shoved out of the arena and deprived of the chance to fight for their rights as human beings.

2

The Great Tranquilizer

Up From Slavery

For more than a quarter of a century one man served as the model Negro in all of the United States. His autobiography, *Up From Slavery,* was required reading in hundreds of one-room Negro schools. Three Presidents visited the industrial school in Alabama where this one-time slave tried to teach the sons and daughters of slaves the dignity of working with one's hands and the importance of the toothbrush and the daily bath. Harvard and Dartmouth gave him honorary degrees; Queen Victoria had him to tea.

But by 1945, when Booker T. Washington was enshrined in the Hall of Fame—the first and only Negro so honored,—he no longer was a figure of gleaming inspiration to his people. By then, in fact, most Negroes were in revolt against everything for which he had been acclaimed.

16

Why this abrupt shift? What made Booker T. Washington the dominant Negro leader in the first place? Why did the years after his death bring so sharp a Negro revulsion against him?

A single speech rocketed Washington to national fame. He was only thirty-nine years old when he rose on a blazing hot September afternoon in 1895 to deliver the most important speech any American Negro had ever made.

Washington had lobbied for this opportunity to address the Cotton States International Exposition in Atlanta. He had appeared before a Congressional committee to urge a federal appropriation to help finance the exposition, terming it the first real opportunity to exhibit the advances made by both races in the South since the Civil War's end. He became the logical choice to deliver one of the opening day addresses as "a representative of Negro enterprise and Negro civilization."

Accounts of the speech tell of the burst of applause that greeted Washington when he urged his fellow Negroes to "cast down your bucket where you are" and make friends "in every manly way" with white neighbors. But his white audience went into a "delirium of applause"—men tossed hats into the air, women stood on chairs, cheering and waving their handkerchiefs—when Washington thrust his right hand high above his head and with his five fingers stretched wide apart, declared: "In all things that are purely social we can be separate as the fingers, yet one as the hand in all things essential to mutual progress."

Seated among the newsmen, Clark Howell, of the Atlanta *Constitution,* turned to James Creelman, of the New York

World, and exclaimed, "That man's speech is the beginning of a moral revolution in America: it is a platform upon which blacks and whites can stand with full justice to each other." Impressed, Creelman, in his dispatch to the *World,* termed Washington's address "an oration that marks a new epoch in the history of the South."

To us today it may seem strange that Washington's words and his five outstretched fingers should have touched off a demonstration of jubilation that might have greeted news of an armistice or the signing of a peace treaty. To the South, though, Washington's speech was just that— an offer of peace and capitulation in the raging racial war.

In renouncing agitation for social equality as "the extremist folly" Washington was accepting defeat for the Negroes in their first effort to put freedom into reality. In effect, he was asking for the best terms that the white South would yield to the black man. In later years other Negro leaders came to denounce his "Atlanta Compromise" and charge that "the white man had raised up Washington to keep the Negro docile and dumb."

But did Washington have any other choice of action?

Two facts must be considered:

First, by 1895 the Negro had long been abandoned by his Northern abolitionist friends.

Second, on their own the Negroes lacked the means with which to fight for their rights.

In those years nine in every ten Negroes still subsisted in the South, some as owners of skimpy acreages but the majority as impoverished sharecroppers. In writing his reminiscences of the period one Southern editor recalled that these croppers were paid "on the same basis that the farm mule is paid—he is given shelter, usually of the most indifferent quality, and an abundance of coarse provender."

A Negro boy born in 1895 had a life expectancy of only 32 years, compared with 46 years for a white male child. Hardly half the Negroes could read or write. In South Carolina schools for Negroes stayed open only 67 days in the year; in Virginia, 120 days. During the three years before Washington made his Atlanta speech a Negro was lynched in the South once every three days.

Emancipation had left most Negroes almost completely dependent on the federal government. Still no program of Negro assistance was set up by President Rutherford B. Hayes when he withdrew the last federal troops from the South as part of the bargain that gave him the tenant's lease on the White House in the disputed Hayes-Tilden election.

Hayes and his fellow Republicans were dreaming of an alliance between men of property in the North and the South. In that scheme of things, Hayes wrote a friend, "As to the South, the let alone policy seems now to be the true course." In another letter he wrote, "Time, time is the great cure-all."

Although less sanguine, President James Garfield pursued the same policy. Shortly after he took office, in 1881, he confided to a friend, "Time is the only cure for the South's difficulties. In what shape it will come, if it comes at all, is not clear."

But if the North had no racial program, the white South did have one. With the hated Yankee "bluebellies" gone, the dominant Southerners set about systematically relegating the Negro "to his place," establishing a segregated caste system under which every black person, denied even the dignity of being called Mr. or Mrs., would be held inferior to any white man.

This process of disfranchisement and Jim Crowism required more than twenty years to complete and in those years Booker T. Washington's career makes strange reading. At times he appears a truly heroic figure, patiently telling his Tuskegee students that the way to win the white man's respect was "to do common things in an uncommon way" —this while Southern politicians were ranting that "the Negro is akin to the monkey" and Negroes are "an ignorant and debased and debauched race."

But at other times Washington's career reads like a mocking satire. "My faith is that reforms in the South will come from within," he kept repeating even as each new year brought further indignities and repressions.

In 1881 Washington borrowed $437 to buy the land that became the site of Tuskegee. The school was opened on July 4 in an abandoned church with holes in its roof. When it rained a student had to hold an umbrella over Washington's head as he held class.

By 1882, with the erection of two small temporary buildings, the umbrella could be put away. That same year, though, South Carolina instituted its "Eight Box Ballot Law," designed to confuse Negro voters. For each office being voted on, a different ballot box was required. If a voter dropped his ballot into the wrong box—to bewilder the illiterate Negroes the boxes were often shuffled—his vote was voided.

In 1883 Washington scored a double triumph. The first permanent structure was erected on Tuskegee's campus. Then, after three heartrending failures, the Tuskegee students succeeded in manufacturing bricks. It gratified Washington that white people "from miles around" came to buy these bricks.

But 1883 was also the year in which the U.S. Supreme Court declared unconstitutional the Civil Rights Act of 1875, which had assured Negroes "full and equal enjoyment" of hotels, inns, theaters, trains and other public accommodations—a more sweeping guarantee than was proposed by the Kennedy administration eighty years later.

Of this decision, which cleared away the legal barriers to Jim Crow legislation, one Negro editor, T. Thomas Fortune, wrote that it made "Negroes feel as if they had been baptized in ice water."

Booker T. Washington had some friends up north. In 1889 Congress allotted Tuskegee 25,000 acres of mineral lands in northern Alabama. But a year later this same Congress, to gain Southern support for a tariff increase, killed a bill which would have protected Negro voting rights. As if responding to the cue, Mississippi in 1890 became the first Southern state to enact a poll tax and "educational" tests to deny Negroes the right to vote.

Most of Tuskegee's graduates were going out into the

South as teachers in rural schools and, as Washington wrote, "we wanted to be careful not to educate our students out of sympathy with agricultural life."

He took pride in the fact that the students built all of Tuskegee's buildings, made their own furniture, their own wagons, their own carts, did their own blacksmithing and harness making. "We ask help for nothing that we can do for ourselves," Washington proudly told the National Education Association. "Nothing is bought that the students can produce."

This emphasis on rural self-sufficiency and plantation skills has caused some historians to wonder about Washington's sense of history. For these were the years in which the South was stumbling into the machine age and casting the mold of employment by race which was to stand to this day.

Textile mills, in particular, were being erected at a feverish pace to provide work for the landless, illiterate whites. Often the funds to build these mills were raised at revival meetings at which ministers pictured the mills—from which all Negroes were to be excluded—as the white man's "escape from competition with the blacks."

Even after Tuskegee's finances no longer required it, Washington continued to stress self-sufficiency and land-ownership as the highest of Negro goals. Did Washington, in emphasizing these premachine skills and rural virtues, fail to recognize the direction in which the South's economy was moving? Or, since the Negro was being walled out of the South's newer economic activities, was the Tuskegee educator trying to demonstrate that the Negro still could improve his lot, even if he had to stand alone?

Separate but Unequal

In adopting his conciliatory, submissive policy Washington was bidding for the support of the more "aristocratic," upper-class whites in the South. His Atlanta speech, in fact, paraphrased the views of that much-publicized spokesman for the "New South," Henry Grady, who had often talked of an alliance of "the better elements" in both races.

To Grady the indispensable requirement for such an alliance was "that whites and blacks must walk together in separate paths. . . . As near as may be, these paths should be equal but separate—they must be now and always."

In 1896 the Supreme Court made this "separate but equal" doctrine the law of the land by deciding, in *Plessy* v. *Ferguson,* that if separate facilities were equal segregation did not deprive citizens of equal protection of the law under the Fourteenth Amendment. This doctrine, which legalized segregation, was to stand for fifty-eight years minus one day.

On May 18, 1896, the case of *Plessy* v. *Ferguson* was decided. On May 17, 1954, the Supreme Court reversed that decision.

Had the South lived up to this "separate but equal" doctrine, racial relations might have taken a different turn. But the white Southerners soon made it clear that they were determined to have the decision read "separate but unequal." Nor did the aristocratic whites, to whom Washington had looked for help, do anything to check the process.

Actually whatever hope might have existed for political aid from the more conservative Southerners was wrecked in the Populist agitations of the late 1880's and the 1890's. In state after state these agrarian radicals challenged the control of the conservatives and tried to sweep the South into political alliance with the agrarian West rather than with the industrial East.

In 1892, bidding boldly to break the conservative hold on the votes of Southern Negroes, the Populists denounced lynch law and called for the defense of the Negro's political rights.

Tom Watson, the leader of Southern Populism, promised Negroes, "if you stand up for your rights and manhood, if you stand shoulder to shoulder with us in this fight" the People's party will "wipe out the color line and put every man on his citizenship irrespective of color." But in the black belt counties, where most Negroes lived, the conservative planters marched their croppers to the polls and outvoted the Populists.

It was during the recoil that followed the defeat of Populism, in successive constitutional conventions, that the white South wrote the ground rules for the Southern arena. Neither the Populists nor the conservatives were interested in a really democratic political structure. They were too ridden with fears—of the North, of the Negro, of one another—to open the future to freely competitive energies.

Their dominant concerns seem to have been to exclude the Negro from political life and to construct a solid white front against possible Northern interference. Inevitably the arena they set up was one in which new social forces would be able to register their influence only with difficulty and in which hardly any economic or political issue could be fought out equitably or even openly.

On the very day that Washington was delivering his Atlanta speech a constitutional convention in South Carolina was meeting to consider ways of barring the Negro from voting. Far from slowing down this move, Washington's speech was cited in later convention sessions as an argument justifying disfranchisement.

In 1898, when Louisiana was preparing to disfranchise the Negro, Washington tried again to slow the action. He and T. Thomas Fortune worked throughout one night drafting a public appeal which argued that "the Negro does not object to an educational or property test but let the law be so clear that no one will be tempted to prejudice and degrade himself by putting one interpretation on it for the white man and another for the black man." This appeal was ignored.

Still Washington never stopped crediting white Southerners with nobler intentions. In *Up From Slavery*, which was serialized in the *Outlook* late in 1900, he wrote:

"Despite superficial and temporary signs which might lead one to entertain a contrary opinion, there was never a time I felt more hopeful for the race than at the present. . . . The outside world does not know, neither can it appreciate, the struggle that is constantly going on in the hearts of both the Southern white people and their former slaves to free themselves from racial prejudice."

Yet earlier that year North Carolina had joined the disfranchisement procession; Georgia had Jim Crowed its streetcars; South Carolina, Arkansas and Georgia had turned the Democratic primary into an exclusively "white primary."

In 1901 Washington was invited to the White House by Theodore Roosevelt, who asked him to stay to dinner. Southern newspapers and politicians exploded in frenzy. South Carolina's "Pitchfork Ben" Tillman, then in the U.S. Senate, declared that "the action of President Roosevelt in entertaining that nigger will necessitate our killing a thousand niggers in the South before they learn their place again."

The fury of anti-Negro feeling in those years, as C. Vann Woodward has written, seems to defy rational explanation. Perhaps it was because the South at that time was a cruel and brutalizing arena for the white man as well. With labor in surplus everywhere, the white supremacists were determined to reserve for their race what job opportunities and economic resources were available.

"To the degree that you close the ballotbox," for Negroes, Washington had begged "open the schoolhouses." But Southern legislatures were unwilling or unable to appropriate funds for both Negro and white schools. Between 1870 and 1910 South Carolina averaged $9.65 a year for schooling a white child—only $1.09 for a Negro child.

In Mississippi in 1904 James K. Vardaman was inaugurated governor after a campaign in which he stumped the state arguing against "the monstrous folly of filling the head of the nigger with useless learning."

When some Northern philanthropists, interested in Negro colleges, stopped off at Atlanta after a visit to Tuskegee, Governor Allen D. Chandler announced, "We can attend to the education of the darky in the South without the aid of these Yankees. . . . I do not believe in higher education of the darky. He should be taught trades, but when he is taught the fine arts he gets educated above his caste and that makes him unhappy."

In time the South did begin spending more on Negro schools, but as late as 1916 Martin Luther King's father could get no more than four years' schooling in rural Georgia and left for Atlanta.

And so the process of rigging the Southern arena against the Negro went on. In agriculture Negroes remained the main source of labor but in industry the general rule was to assign them the jobs left after the white men had been taken care of or to give Negroes work that white men wouldn't do. Even trades like barbering, in which Negroes had traditionally served both races, were taken over by whites.

These discriminations did not extend into federal employment. Wherever they could, Negroes, like Walter White's father, found work in the post office.

By 1906 six more states had Jim Crowed streetcars, while seven more—Florida, Tennessee, Alabama, Mississippi, Louisiana, Texas and Kentucky—had adopted the "white primary."

Still, in the preface to his biography of Frederick Douglass, which was published in 1906, Booker T. Washington could write: "We are at present in a period of construction and readjustments. Many of the animosities engendered by the conflicts and controversies of half a century ago still survive. . . . But changes are rapidly coming about that will remove, or at least greatly modify, these lingering animosities."

Washington was having considerable success in gaining the support of wealthy Northern capitalists. Some of these industrialists were impressed by his faith in the simple virtues of hard work, thrift and self-reliance. Others saw in his program of industrial education a means of ensuring the South an ample supply of pliable labor "that is almost a stranger to strikes."

Tuskegee's assets had grown to where they exceeded $3 million. Andrew Carnegie had donated a library plus $600,000. Other Tuskegee buildings bore such names as Rockefeller, George Eastman, Henry Rogers (of Standard Oil) and Collis B. Huntington (of the Southern Pacific). Almost it seemed that the benefactions to Tuskegee increased in generosity as more and more of the Negro rights in the South were lost.

Washington himself had become far more than the mere head of Tuskegee. Both Theodore Roosevelt and William Howard Taft consulted him on virtually all Negro political appointments and even on some white appointments in the South. Northern philanthropic organizations usually cleared with Washington before granting requests for funds to other Negro institutions in the South. Many Negro newspapers throughout the country were subsidized from Tuskegee.

But this contrast between Washington's eminence and the Negro's sinking political fortunes began to trouble some of the more educated Negroes in the North. Soon their voices were raised in protest against "the Tuskegee Machine."

In Boston, when Washington rose to speak at a colored church, he was hissed vigorously by some younger Negroes, led by William Monroe Trotter, who edited a crusading Negro weekly. So stormy was the uproar that thirty-five policemen were called in to restore quiet and Trotter was arrested.

More significant was the attack on Washington by William Edward Burghardt Du Bois, in *The Souls of Black Folk,* published in the spring of 1903. Although Du Bois was then teaching sociology at Atlanta University, he was Northern-born and had not known slavery personally.

Expressing "deep regret, sorrow and apprehension at the ascendancy" of this "one recognized spokesman of his ten million followers," Du Bois accused Washington of wanting to train "black boys and girls forever to be hewers of wood and drawers of water."

An intellectual by temperament, Du Bois had his own prescription for Negro salvation. He contended that "the Negro race like all races is going to be saved by its exceptional men or its 'Talented Ten.' " To train the leaders of a struggling people, he felt, the "best and most capable of their youth must be schooled in the colleges and universities of the land."

Washington's emphasis on industrial education, Du Bois

charged, dried up the funds needed for this higher education of more militant leaders. But his chief quarrel with Washington seems to have been the latter's policy of "no open agitation." Du Bois blamed Washington for the disfranchisement of the Negro and demanded that Negro leaders "insist continually, in season and out of season, that voting is necessary to modern manhood."

To mobilize opposition to Washington, Du Bois in 1905 issued a personal call for a conference which came to be known as the "Niagara Movement" because it met on the Canadian side of Niagara Falls (no hotels being open to Negroes on the American side). The next year, for the Niagara group's first national meeting, Du Bois picked the most militant sounding location he could think of, Harpers Ferry, where John Brown had died. There a series of resolutions were drawn up including one which declared:

"We will not be satisfied to take one jot or tittle less than our full manhood rights. We claim for ourselves every single right that belongs to a freeborn American, political, civil and social, and until we get these rights we will never cease to protest and assail the ears of America."

The next morning at dawn Du Bois and his followers marched barefoot to the engine house where John Brown had made his last stand and, as the sun rose, they sang "The Battle Hymn of the Republic."

Du Bois' attacks drew little attention in the general press but they did impress the small band of white intellectuals who had a special concern for Negroes. In 1910 an editorial in Oswald Garrison Villard's New York *Evening Post* criticized Washington's role as "political boss of his race" and urged Negroes to fight to prevent the "tightening of chains that must some day be broken if this is to be a republic in more ways than name."

Perhaps because of these criticisms, Washington did become somewhat more outspoken against segregation and lynching in his later years.

In 1912 in *Century Magazine* he asked, "Is the Negro Having a Fair Chance?" and replied with an unmistakable "No." On the basis of this article the Chicago *Defender* assumed that Washington had reversed his previous position and congratulated him on his conversion.

Washington's last public words, published in the *New Republic* in 1915 shortly after his death, condemned segregation as "an injustice inviting other injustices and embittering the Negro and dissolving the moral fiber of the white man."

Epitaph for the White Man

How are we to interpret Washington's career? Was he little more than a submissive "Uncle Tom" selling the Negro short or was he, as Roy Wilkins has suggested, "a master politician" who "envisioned complete equality as the goal for his people . . . a shrewd man, thoroughly in tune with his time, he appeared to be an appeaser and did his great work under that protective cloak."

Actually it is doubtful that anything Washington might have said or done could have slowed the process of disfranchisement.

Constant policing of the South by troops would have

been needed to protect the Negro's rights. Northern whites, primarily concerned with "binding up the wounds" caused by the Civil War, shrank from any such prospect.

One wonders, in fact, whether the deeper significance of Washington's career does not lie in what it reveals about white America. Throughout his career Washington searched for a basis on which Negroes and whites could live in amity rather than enmity. His considerable energies and talents were given over to a single-minded hunt for friends of the Negro, wherever they might be found, and to utilize whatever residue of good feeling there might be in the white race for bettering the Negro's lot.

How much—or how little—he was able to accomplish reflected less his own beliefs and convictions than what white America was ready to yield to the Negro at that time. The stone on Washington's grave might well read, "Here lies the best the white man could do" for the Negro at that juncture of American history.

In *My Larger Education,* written in 1911, Washington explained that he had felt his life mission was to find some means of resolving the antagonisms of the Southern white man, the Northern white man and the Negro.

Certainly for the Southern Negro Washington kept alive the hope of a better day coming. The fact that he could be entertained by Presidents and royalty must have stirred Negro pride. It was also reassuring to Negroes to be told that industry, virtue and thrift would triumph eventually over Jim Crowism.

Ray Stannard Baker recalled that, in traveling through

the South, "Wherever I found a prosperous Negro enterprise, a thriving business place, a good home, there I was almost sure to find Booker T. Washington's picture over the fireplace or a little framed motto expressing his gospel of work and service."

The whites in both South and North also needed reassurance. Northerners, who had abandoned the Negro politically, could salve their consciences by telling themselves that the Negro did not feel betrayed, that he had not given up in despair but recognized that he was "not yet ready" and that with time his lot would improve.

For Southern whites Washington was immensely useful in fulfilling their need for a show of paternalism. Washington was one Negro the South could be "nice" to, even as later Southerners would boast how "I always help my nigger friends" out of scrapes.

Washington, in short, was truly the great tranquilizer for his era—for the Southerners who rigged things so the Negro would have little chance, for the Northern whites who didn't want to fight the Negro's battle, and for the Negroes who couldn't fight back themselves.

But tranquillity exacts its price. It was in those tranquilizing years that the South built the structure of segregation which we now are trying to dismantle with such agony and pain.

How one generation spent the time given it left a heavy mortgage indeed for future generations to pay off.

3

Black Nationalism

The Negro Moves North

It was inevitable that the Negroes, given the opportunity and power, would try to rewrite the history of Booker T. Washington's years. In George Orwell's totalitarian society of 1984 rewriting history was a fairly simple process. Events that should not have happened or the names of persons who had been vaporized would be deleted and new histories would be published. Dropped into "memory holes" that led to furnaces, the records of the past ceased to exist.

But in actual life history commands its armies of loyalists and a system of fortifications that extend into every institution of society. If the stakes are high enough, rewriting history—or the refusal to do so—can become political and social war.

34

Segregation was instituted by the South itself, with most Northerners looking away as if it were none of their affair. Perhaps with poetic irony the struggle to undo segregation has generated an ever-deeper involvement for more and more of the nation. Where Hayes and Garfield could leave it to "time alone" to correct the Negro's plight, Eisenhower, Kennedy and Johnson were compelled to use troops. What only a few years ago still seemed a remote and abstract issue has steadily become more and more a conflict that creeps ever deeper into our daily lives.

The process by which the whole nation has been drawn into this racial strife still is only dimly perceived. Yet, like all conflicts that build up over the years, it has acquired its own distinctive dynamics, which seem to be propelling us along a fixed course. If we are to regain some control over the future we need to understand how this pattern of involvement took shape.

One part of the story can be grasped quite quickly by a glance at a simple statistical table which shows the leaping increases in the proportion of the Negro population living outside the South.

When World War I cut off immigration, Northern industry turned southward for the labor it needed. Between 1916 and 1923 roughly a million Negroes were drawn north. With this migration the Negro moved into a new arena in which he could at last fight for his rights. And as the number of Negroes in the North has risen their militancy has mounted steadily.

Even as late as 1940 more than three of every four Negroes still remained in the South. But by 1960 a full 40 percent were in the North and on the Pacific Coast. Before 1970 the proportion is expected to pass the 50-50 mark.

But this nearly fourfold increase in the Northern Negro population since 1920 tells only part of the story. Before the Negro could turn upon the South to right the wrongs he

TABLE I.   *Rise in Negroes Outside South*

	% of Total	No. of Negroes
1900	*10*	*1,647,377*
1910	*11*	*1,899,654*
1920	*15*	*2,407,371*
1930	*21*	*3,483,746*
1940	*23*	*3,986,606*
1950	*32*	*5,989,543*
1960	*40*	*9,009,470*

Source: U.S. Census.

or his parents had suffered there he had to win some degree of acceptance in the North.

In the course of his struggle he went through a succession of transformations. At first self-conflict locked him in racial frustration which sought release in an almost theatrical Black Nationalism. Then slowly this racial intensity was subdued as the Negro found other interests which allied him to white society. But abruptly, following the Supreme Court's desegregation decision, his racialism flared anew in militant bargaining whose aims and ends remain uncertain.

Will this new racial militancy tear apart both the Negro and white society? Or will its belligerence be drained away by the unifying interests of whites and blacks?

A Split Personality

Almost from the first day he stepped off the train in Chicago, Detroit or New York the newly arrived Negro found himself torn by conflicting emotions. One Southern migrant, asked about his first impressions of Chicago, recalled:

"When I got on the streetcars and saw colored people sitting by white people I just held my breath. I thought any minute they would start something. Then I saw nobody noticed it. I just thought this was a real place for colored people."

But another newcomer remembered: "I was completely lost. A friend was to meet me but didn't. Finally my friend came. I was afraid to sleep the first night—so much noise. I thought the cars would finally stop running so I could rest."

In the South the Negro knew his "place"—the white man permitted him no doubt on that score. But in the North the Negro discovered that his status had still to be defined. Nor did it seem to fit any clear or even fixed pattern.

Back in the black belt counties of Alabama cotton chopping had paid from 50 cents to $1 a day; in the North unskilled labor brought $3 to $8 a day. However, if most Negroes were handling more money than they had ever seen before they still lived in segregated ghettos. When they tried to move into better neighborhoods they often met with bombings.

In those war years the jobs that Negroes were drawn into were mainly the sweaty, unskilled work that earlier had gone to European immigrants—in steel mills and meat-packing plants, in auto factories and Pullman yards. On these jobs Negroes and whites worked side by side, which would have been unthinkable in the South. But in many of these industries racial tension was an unseen foreman, pitting white and Negro workers against each other. When strikes took place they often exploded into murderous race riots.

In short, almost everything about this new urban arena tended to give the Northern Negro a split personality. Among both the mass of Negroes and their leaders there developed a bitter inner conflict, which has continued to this day.

Essentially the clash has been between acceptance and alienation, between the spurrings to adopt the white man's ways in order to be treated as his equal and the shame and anger over being denied that equality, shames and angers which impel Negroes to lash out against almost everything the white man symbolizes.

The torments and agonies of this conflict were reflected vividly each week in the columns of the Chicago *Defender,* which had been started by Robert Abbott on a proverbial shoestring and had been built into the Negro newspaper with the heaviest circulation in the nation.

Born of slave parents near Savannah, Ga., in 1868, Abbott was sensitive and vain. He liked to be seen carrying a gold-headed cane and wearing a top hat, cutaway coat, striped trousers and spats. But he edited the *Defender* almost literally like a man trying to break out of his skin.

Intensely black in complexion, he hated the color black. Roi Ottley, his biographer, wrote that "he avoided black as a color for clothes and rarely appeared in public accompanied by a black woman." (His first wife was so light she was mistaken for white.)

He urged Negro fraternities to "whiteball" rather than "blackball" anyone being denied membership. He even barred the word "Negro" from the *Defender's* columns, using terms such as "race man" and "race woman" instead.

Through the *Defender* Abbott tried to purge "the race" of habits and practices that he considered demeaning. One crusade was directed against the "African dodge 'em" game in which carnival visitors heaved balls at the head of a Negro, while the barker called, "Hit the coon and win a cigar!" To the *Defender* Negroes who sought this work were "criminals against the race."

Abbott also campaigned to lift the efficiency of Negro workers and to improve their public conduct. He encouraged Negro parents to send their daughters to finishing schools where they could learn "fine manners" and foreign languages.

But if one issue of the *Defender* urged Negroes to be "genteel" another reeked with hate-curdling stories of racial outrages, printed under sensational red-inked headlines. Some of the more lurid of these reports were of incidents that never happened.

If it was a dull week for news, J. Hockley Smiley, the *Defender's* managing editor, would lubricate his imagination with jiggers of gin and manufacture reports of lynchings, rapes and sundry other crimes against innocent Negroes in the southern hinterlands, often in towns that could not be found on any map.

These "race" stories were frequently tied to some crusade that Abbott was pushing. Perhaps his most famous effort was his "The Great Northern Drive" to get Negroes to come out of the South.

Much of the *Defender*'s circulation was in the South and beginning in 1916 the *Defender* devoted considerable space to the job opportunities that awaited Negroes in the North. One typical advertisement ran:

"3000 laborers to work on railroad. Factory hires all race help. More positions open than men for them."

Reinforcing such advertisements would be editorial and news stories aimed at demolishing arguments that might be raised in the South against coming north. It was not unusual to read in the *Defender* a description of the South as a land "of blight, of murdered kin, of deflowered womanhood, wrecked homes, strangled ambitions, make-believe virginity, trumped up charges, lonely graves, where owls hoot and where friends dare not go."

In recent years the South has encouraged Negroes to move north, but during World War I their labor still was needed to work the fields of cotton, rice and sugar cane, to man the sawmills, to tap the turpentine trees.

To halt the northward exodus, some Southern communities forbade the sale of the *Defender,* confiscating copies on display in stores. Labor agents recruiting Negroes for Northern industry were required to pay heavy licensing fees, Macon, Ga., putting its fee at a prohibitive $25,000 a year.

In some cities policemen patrolled the railroad stations arresting Negroes who were waiting for northbound trains or destroying their tickets. At Greenville, Miss., trains were stopped and Negroes on board were taken off.

When Southern newspapers began headlining stories of the cold Northern winters the *Defender* retorted in its columns, "To die from the bite of frost is far more glorious than that of the mob."

For some years Abbott served as the principal voice of protest for the Negro masses. Then, in 1919, a new Black Moses appeared, energetic, belligerent and eloquent, who stirred the imagination of his people as no other Negro leader ever has.

"A little fat black man, ugly but with intelligent eyes and a big head" was how Du Bois described Marcus Garvey. Born in Jamaica in 1887, Garvey had worked as a typesetter and printer but had little formal education, a lack he felt keenly. One of his favorite poses was to be photographed in academic cap and gown. Often he tacked after his name the initials D.C.L. to suggest that he held an honorary degree.

Most Negro writers have pictured the Garvey movement, which raised $10 million from his followers before it collapsed, as little more than a grand show, a colorful demonstration of Negro showmanship and mass appeal.

Yet Garvey's movement holds lasting significance. In truth, it has never died out of the Negro consciousness. His was the voice of alienation which somehow managed to bring together into one package the main ideas that surge through the mind of the Negro when he feels spurned by white society. Much as the NAACP has symbolized the struggle to gain the white man's respect and acceptance, Garvey stands for the frustration of that goal.

Ostensibly he preached "back to Africa," but actually he stimulated Negroes to a fierce pride of race by urging the rejection of everything the white man stood for.

Where Abbott hated the color black, Garvey glorified it. Ridiculing efforts at assimilation with whites, he extolled black skins and contended that the Negro could expect no progress in a country dominated by white men. The black man needed his own government, with his own president in the Black House and a "Black God in Heaven." His followers paraded through Harlem bearing aloft pictures of a Black Madonna and a Black Christ Child.

He set up a Black Star steamship line, which was to trade with black peoples all over the world; he organized a string of Negro businesses—a chain of cooperative groceries, a laundry, hotel, a tailor and a dress shop; also a factory which manufactured black dolls.

This emphasis on "Black Nationalism" and racial purity brought Garvey into sharp conflict with almost all the other Negro leaders and particularly with Du Bois, then the editor of the NAACP organ, the *Crisis*. In part theirs was a clash of personalities—a mulatto Brahmin against a Black Agitator—but even their personal characteristics reflected the fact that each man symbolized a quite different stream of Negro living.

Du Bois represented the thin middle-class crust that had developed among Negroes in the North before the mass influx from the South. The outward badge of their social

standing was lightness of skin, which meant that some
parent or grandparent had been white. Usually these middle-
class elements had received a fair degree of education and
enjoyed economic opportunities denied darker-skinned
Negroes.

Du Bois himself boasted that mixed with his Negro blood
was "a strain of French, a bit of Dutch and thank God
not a drop of Anglo-Saxon blood." His great-great-grand-
father had been freed after fighting briefly for the colonial
forces in the Revolutionary War. As a child in Great Bar-
rington, Mass., where he was born, Du Bois had experienced
little racial discrimination. After attending Fisk and gradu-
ating from Harvard he had studied in Germany, returning
with a goatee, spats and a cane.

To his biographer, Frances Broderick, Du Bois looked
"like a Spanish aristocrat . . . with his well-trimmed goatee
. . . proud, outspoken, he never forgot for a moment his
educational background . . . he held aloof from the Negro
masses."

Garvey, on the other hand, voiced the feelings of the
raw, uncouth, often ignorant Negroes who had flooded into
the Northern cities. Being extremely black himself, he at
times seemed more resentful of mulattoes than of whites.
He taunted Du Bois and other light-skinned NAACP
leaders as "mongrels."

"I feel the spell of Africa on me," Du Bois once wrote
in conjuring up dreams of an independent African nation.
He had organized the first Pan-African Congress, which
met in Paris in 1920. But nothing much came of the Con-

gress except some speeches and resolutions.

Garvey, in contrast, took the skeleton dream of a free Africa and gave it the flesh and regalia of showmanship. Boldly proclaiming his intention to "liberate the 400 million Negroes of the world," he had himself crowned provisional president of this new African government. He then proceeded to establish his own black court, appointing dukes and duchesses who were honored with decorations from the Distinguished Order of Ethiopia or the Sublime Order of the Nile. He organized a Corps of Black Cross nurses and a brightly uniformed African Legion, which hinted that someday Africa might be freed by force.

At meetings and in parades Garvey's followers sang their own national anthem: "Ethiopia, Thou Land of Our Fathers." They proudly waved their own black, green and red flag (black for Negro skin, green for Negro hopes, red for Negro blood)—the same colors that Kenya adopted when it became independent in 1963.

All this pomp and splendor was heady inspiration to former slaves and offspring of slaves who had never known much to be proud of. Many joined Garvey's Universal Negro Improvement Association, paying 35 cent dues a week. They bought Garvey's newspaper, the *Negro World,* which was printed in English, French and Spanish. They turned out by the thousands to watch Garvey's parades.

Nearly 40,000 Negroes purchased more than 155,000 shares of stock in the Black Star Line. Four ships were bought, three actually going to sea—the first ships in modern history to sail under a black captain and a black crew.

But Garvey was no steamship operator. On its first cruise to the West Indies the *Yarmouth* carried a cargo of whiskey, much of which was stolen. The ship was old, having been built the same year Garvey was born. Repairs ran so high that the *Yarmouth* had to be sold to pay off creditors.

Two other ships were beached for extensive repairs. When the fourth ship never sailed Garvey was indicted for mail fraud and convicted. In 1927, after serving more than two years in Atlanta, his sentence was commuted and he was deported. He died in London in 1940.

When Garvey was arrested Arthur Brisbane protested that "it was like jailing a rainbow." Garvey's more kindly critics termed him a "poor organizer"; the less kindly ones labeled him a "downright charlatan" or "a Jamaican vagabond." He left little tangible behind him, nothing like Tuskegee or the writings of Du Bois. The one crusade Garvey won—to get the word "Negro" capitalized—is rarely associated with his name.

It is also doubtful that any appreciable number of Garvey's followers ever seriously considered leaving this country. Feeling themselves American, many asked, "How can we go back to Africa when we never were there?"

Still Garvey's venture must be looked upon as much more than escapist theatricals. It is intriguing to note how many of the themes of Garveyism as a rejection of white society persist in Negro thinking and feeling. The glorification of the color black, the emotional identification with African independence, efforts to organize Negro owned and operated business, drives to "buy black," retreats into self-segregation—all of these agitations were first brought forward by Garvey.

The Black Muslims are an angrier version of Garveyism, tinging their glorification of the black race with open hatred of the white "devil." Elijah Muhammad's attacks on Christianity as "hypocritical" echo Garvey's aides who exhorted Negroes to "erase the white gods from your heart" and "worship God through the eyes of Ethiopia." Although Garvey, a Catholic, never repudiated Christianity fully, he did criticize it as the religion that white men "preach and will not practice."

In almost every Negro the craving to reject the white man seems to battle constantly with the hunger to be accepted by him. The Negro himself is unable, of course, to resolve this self-conflict, since he cannot either spurn white society fully or win its full acceptance. Whenever the stresses of ineffective integration rise, then the Garveylike side of his split personality, with its search for a positive black identity, gains ascendancy. Then, in the words of E. Franklin Frazier, Negroes demand to be "Somebody among white people who have said they were Nobody."

Malcolm X and other Negroes like James Baldwin and Le Roi Jones have interjected a new note into this schizophrenic conflict—the threat of violence. Reflecting, as it does, the rise in Negro expectations, this threat has had its bargaining value. Before his assassination, in fact, Malcolm X served as a kind of "wicked partner" to the Negro Revolution, a sinister, hate-preaching figure who could be pointed to as the bloodier alternative towards which the Negro masses might turn if the demands of less zealous Negro leaders were not met.

Finale in Africa

For Du Bois the collapse of the "Back to Africa" bubble was a political victory but it was to prove a hollow, ironic one. In battling Garvey, Du Bois and the NAACP had reaffirmed their fundamental faith in the concept of gaining equal rights with other Americans. But this goal remained as tantalizing to realize as Garvey's.

All through the 1920's Du Bois sought vainly to find an ally for the Negro among other crusading groups—prohibitionists, suffragettes, labor unions. But none of these groups was prepared to hitch its aspirations to the racial star. He flirted with the Democratic party. By 1930 he was scraping the bottom of the political barrel with talk of a third party which would embrace all the politically "homeless voters" in the country.

Much of Du Bois' frustrations reflected the fact that he was trying to rush the workings of time. His writings were important in stimulating a spirit of protest among Negroes and in awakening white society to indignation over lynching and other antihuman abuses inflicted upon Negroes. But at the time there existed no basis for effective integration of the mass of Negroes and whites.

Among the Negroes themselves too wide a gap separated the intellectual from the masses. Nor did Negroes share any unified sense of economic interest in their dealings with white people.

Domestic maids might resent the overbearing ways of their white mistresses and echo the angers voiced by Countee Cullen:

> She thinks that even up in heaven
> Her class lies late and snores
> While poor black cherubs rise at seven
> To do celestial chores.

But most Negroes felt themselves in economic competition with the white man and saw their interests as more closely allied with wealthier, paternalistic employers than with white workers at the same occupational level. The link that was missing—to be forged under the New Deal—was a common consciousness of economic class, strong enough to subordinate Negro-white racial antagonism.

In his *The Souls of Black Folk* Du Bois had written eloquently of how "one feels ever his two-ness—an American, a Negro, two souls, two thoughts, two unreconciled strivings; two warring ideals in one dark body, whose dogged strength alone keeps it from being torn asunder."

In his personal struggle with his own "two-ness" Du Bois retreated steadily into a more intensified racialism. The 1920's were years of golden recognition for Negro writers, singers and musicians. Du Bois hailed them as evidence that the development of art and the appreciation of beauty were the distinctive mission of the Negro. He attributed Egyptian art to the Negro blood in the Pharaohs; he argued that the Negroes had brought music to America.

Du Bois was not alone in this glorification of Black Art. James Weldon Johnson, after composing a Negro "national hymn," declared that "The Negro is the creator of the only things artistic that have yet sprung from American soil." But Du Bois pursued this line of thinking more systematically. He urged Negroes to develop their own ethos and culture, separate and apart from the white man. As unemployment increased in the early 1930's, he argued in favor of creating a separate Negro economy inside the United States.

In explaining this proposal Du Bois actually defended segregation. This proved too much for the NAACP leadership, long at odds with Du Bois, and in 1934 he was compelled to resign as editor of the *Crisis*.

Du Bois lived another twenty-nine years, but never again was he a part of the mainstream of Negro striving. By temperament a lone crusader, he searched constantly for a new cause. He repudiated many of his old ideas, including his faith in the leadership of the "Talented Tenth" of Negroes who were coming out of college.

Turning to "peace" as a new crusade, he was drawn into the Stockholm Peace Movement as a Communist decoy. In 1951 he was indicted for failing to register the Peace Information Center as the American agent of a foreign country.

By 1961 he had openly joined the Communist party. The next year, at age ninety-four, he took up permanent residence in Ghana, where he died on the eve of the 1963 March on Washington. The man who had ridiculed Marcus Garvey as "a lunatic or traitor" became perhaps the one American who finally answered Garvey's "Back to Africa" call.

4

The Roosevelt Revolution

Of Emancipation and Machines

Of the key elements in the American electorate Negroes have remained consistently the most loyal of voters. Over the past half century, when major shifts of power have occurred from one party to another, Negroes generally have lagged one election behind the rest of the nation. They broke from their Republican allegiance for Franklin Roosevelt in 1936, not 1932; they swung for Dwight D. Eisenhowever in 1956, not 1952. When control of cities like Philadelphia, Chicago, Pittsburgh and New York changed, Negroes usually were the last to forsake the losing party.

This record of party loyalty contrasts quite sharply with the much-publicized political strategy of Negro leaders, of holding the balance of power in presidential elections by keeping the Negro voter independent of both Democrats and Republicans and ready to shift to whichever bids highest in terms of action on civil rights.

In essence this strategy assumes that the issue of civil rights is the one overriding consideration that governs Negro political thinking. While racial feeling has come to dominate the voting of Negroes in the South (for reasons to be discussed later) it has not been true in the North.

Actually the story of the Negro in Northern politics revolves around his slow acquisition of other than racial interests. It was the development of these other interests — such as the attractions of the big city machine, union membership and the economic appeals of the New Deal — that broke the Negro's Republicanism and moved him into the Democratic party, despite its being the party of his hated political foe, the white Southerner.

For the immediate future the important fact of Negro political life remains the solidarity with which he has dug into the Democratic party. Even before their astonishing 1964 showing — when Negroes voted more than 95 per cent for Johnson — this solidarity had been yielding the Democrats a plurality of a million or more votes in presidential elections. But this solidarity has also helped bring about an upheaval in the voting habits of white Southerners and threatens to change the voting of white voters in the North as well.

That Negroes should now be so deeply entrenched in the Democratic party is all the more astonishing when one recalls how intense was their loyalty to the party of Abraham Lincoln and emancipation. Most Negroes had been raised to agree with Frederick Douglass, the ex-slave and first recognized Negro leader, who preached "The Republican

Party is the ship, all else is the open sea. . . . I would as soon go to hell as vote Democratic."

In the North, however, Negroes soon acquired a second loyalty—to the political machine in the city where they lived. In some cities, like New York, Negroes developed the practice of voting Democratic in local elections and Republican for President. This same split-level loyalty persisted into the New Deal years, when, as in Philadelphia, Negroes continued to vote with the Republican machine in local elections, long after they had turned Democratic in presidential voting.

The Negro's dependence on the political machine has persisted to this day, which raises the question whether Negroes can for long remain independent of those who control City Hall. Possibly because of continued immigration, sizable numbers of Negroes need the services traditionally performed by the machines. In the 1920's and early 1930's there were baskets before Christmas or coalbins to be filled; also help in getting out of knifing scrapes, in raising bail or in finding jobs. In more recent years the big city machine has offered assistance in getting onto the relief or welfare rolls, or into public housing and antipoverty projects.

How strong the pull of the machine was upon the early Negro migrants from the South could be seen in New York City. Tammany Hall had an impressive proslavery reputation to overcome with Negroes. Before the Civil War Tammany henchmen often broke up abolitionist meetings. In 1860 Mayor Fernando Wood used gangs of Tammany repeaters to sweep New York City for Stephen Douglas, with 62,611 votes to Lincoln's 33,311.

When it seemed certain the South would secede, Mayor Wood actually proposed that New York secede from the United States and establish itself as a free and independent city-state so that it could continue to trade with the South.

As late as 1915 fewer than 1,000 Negroes were enrolled as Democrats in the whole city. By 1920, though, the exodus from the South had swelled New York's Negro population to over 150,000. The bulk of the newcomers tended to vote Democratic in local elections. By 1930, when New York's Negro population stood at 327,000, only three of the twenty-two political clubs in the city were still Republican.

This alliance of the Negro with the corrupt political bosses dismayed white reformers but not Negro leaders. In 1925, in an article for the *Crisis,* Du Bois defended Ferdinand Q. Morton, then the Democratic boss of Harlem. Before Morton became the leader of Black Tammany, Du Bois argued, there was not a single Negro on the New York City police force, nor any Negro representatives in the legislative branches of the state or city. By 1925 the city was employing "fifty or more policemen, hundreds of Negro clerks, stenographers, typists, investigators, parole officers, court attendants. One Negro is an alderman; the state legislature includes a Negro."

Morton, Du Bois conceded, "does not attempt to stop all gambling, bootlegging, and prostitution in Harlem. But he does limit these things and protects those who wish to be decent and he has helped make Harlem a far better residence quarter than it used to be."

Similarly, when the Thompson machine in Chicago sent

Oscar De Priest to Washington as the first Northern Negro congressman, Du Bois acknowledged "with bowed head" that it would have been nicer if De Priest stood for virtue. But if he had he never would have been elected. The only organized interest that would support a Negro for Congress was allied with the rule of crime.

The Negro political advance was more rapid in Chicago than in any other city. In part this could be credited to segregation. The fact that virtually all of Chicago's Negroes were crowded into one compact residential area made them the dominant voting force in Chicago's First Congressional District.

In Chicago, as well, the Republican party was torn by factional strife. As "Big Bill" Thompson was to demonstrate, a solid Negro vote could be decisive in winning the GOP nomination for mayor.

Thompson, whose three terms as mayor have been termed among the "worst" in Chicago history, was a showman politician—barkers would entice passers-by into his rallies by shouting "See Big Bill in person"—who played heavily to the ethnic galleries.

He is best known for his anti-British, pro-German repertory. German-Americans then constituted the largest single immigrant bloc in Chicago and Thompson appealed for their votes by opposing America's entry into World War I. He also exploited Irish hatred of England through such antics as accusing the King of England of wanting George Washington's photograph removed from Chicago textbooks.

Still, neither of these performances had the sustained effectiveness of his bid for Negro support. Thompson had started in politics as a "reformer" alderman from the Second Ward — then, as now, the main area of Negro residence in Chicago. The first measure he introduced into the City Council called for a $1,200 appropriation to build a public playground — Chicago's first — in the Negro part of his ward.

While campaigning for mayor in the Negro wards Thompson would refight the Battle of Mobile Bay as he described how his father had served under Admiral Farragut. He liked to sneer at his opponents as "Southern crackers." At one Negro rally he picked up a nephew of De Priest and rested his cheek on the boy's black skin.

He promised Negroes, "I'll give your people jobs." He also told them "if any of you want to shoot craps go ahead and do it. When I'm mayor the police will have something better to do than break up a little friendly crap game." As mayor, Thompson banned the showing of *The Birth of a Nation*, which glorified the Ku Klux Klan. He also passed out so many jobs to Negroes that his opponents often referred to City Hall as "Uncle Tom's Cabin." The Negro voters responded to this political courtship with the affection of a long-neglected spinster. In the 1927 Republican primary the Second Ward gave Thompson a swooning 95 percent of its vote; in the 1931 primary, 91 percent of its vote.

Negro affection for Thompson was strengthened by the Democrats. During the 1927 campaign the Democrats sent calliopes through the streets of white neighborhoods playing "Bye, Bye, Blackbird," while leaflets were distributed showing a trainload of Negroes in Georgia with Thompson as the train engineer over a caption which read: "This train will start for Chicago if Thompson is elected."

By 1931 most of Chicago had wearied of Big Bill and his alliance with the Al Capone mob. But most Negroes still shared the view of one Negro minister who, after listing the gains that Negroes had won under Thompson, declared, "God made just one William Hale Thompson and forgot the mold."

Through all of Chicago Thompson drew only 40 percent of the vote in 1931; but the Negroes in the Second and Third Wards gave him better than 80 percent of their vote.

White and Black Unite

By far the most impressive demonstration of Negro party loyalty, however, came in the 1932 presidential election. No other voting group in the nation had been hit harder by unemployment. Also during much of his administration Herbert Hoover had been widely criticized by Negro newspapers and Negro leaders.

As secretary of the NAACP, Walter White had dubbed Hoover "the man in the lily white house" in protest against Hoover's efforts to court white voters in the South. The NAACP had also organized strong Negro opposition in a successful fight to get the Senate to reject Hoover's nomination of Judge John J. Parker of North Carolina to the Supreme Court.

Still, the 1932 election showed less of a defection among

Negroes than among other groups of Republican voters. In both Chicago and Cleveland nearly a third of all Negro males were jobless. Yet Hoover drew more than three fourths of the vote in the heaviest Negro wards. In Philadelphia, where more than a fourth of the Negro workers were out of work, the colored wards gave Hoover 70 per cent of the vote.

In some cities Roosevelt did manage to cut in appreciably on the Negro's Republican loyalty. Hoover could squeeze out only a bare majority in Detroit's three Negro wards; he lost Harlem's two assembly districts and Pittsburgh's "Hill" wards by a small margin. Robert Vann, publisher of the Pittsburgh *Courier,* had broken openly with the Republicans and had campaigned throughout Pittsburgh urging Negroes to "Go home and turn Lincoln's picture to the wall. The debt has been paid in full."

In the nation as a whole the really big Negro political break came in 1936, as can be seen by Table II. At the time observers credited this astonishing political conversion to work relief provided by the creation of WPA. For Negroes

TABLE II.   *Negro Unemployment and Voting*

	% Negroes Unemployed 1932	% Republican for President of Negro Wards 1932	% Republican for President of Negro Wards 1936
Chicago	30	77	51
Cleveland	33	76	38
Philadelphia	28	73	34
Pittsburgh	25	48	17
Detroit	37	50	25
New York City	24	41	19

WPA did seem to come almost like manna from God. In 1933 more than 2 million Negroes were on relief, one in every six Negro workers. By January of 1935 this number had risen to 3,500,000, or a fifth of the Negro labor force.

In Chicago one Negro preacher climaxed a sermon with the exhortation "Let Jesus lead you and Roosevelt feed you." A blues song recorded at the time chanted:

> Please, Mr. President, listen to what I've got to say:
> You can take away all of the alphabet but please
>   now leave that WPA
> I went to the poll and voted, I know I voted the
>   right way
> So I'm asking you, Mr. President, don't take away
>   that WPA.

But the impact of the New Deal extended far beyond the relief rolls. Nearly every aspect of Negro life was touched—and transformed.

WPA itself, for example, really served as an economic floor for the whole Negro community. As long as a Negro could go on WPA he was not forced to accept work at any wage that might be offered him. Rarely has any single government action so suddenly lifted the economic bargaining power of a whole race.

The CCC camps drew something like 200,000 Negroes off the city streets, 30,000 of them living in integrated camps. PWA funds were allocated to build housing, schools and hospitals for Negroes. The swelling rosters of government employees included a record number of Negro appointees.

More significant perhaps than the increase in the number of Negro appointees was the change in the quality of this patronage. Under Republican Presidents a handful of federal posts had been reserved by tradition for Negroes. Invariably these positions—the recorder of deeds in Washington, D.C., and the register of the Treasury, or as envoys to Haiti, to Liberia and other parts of Africa—were far removed from any concern with domestic Negro problems.

During the first few New Deal years, however, 55 Negroes were named to government posts; by 1940 the number had risen to more than 100. Most of these officeholders were relatively young college graduates, reflecting the expansion of the Negro middle class that had continued to grow even during the depression. These years also marked a broadening of Negro leadership. In place of the earlier emphasis on one or two national spokesmen a whole corps of leaders stepped forward to make the improvement of race relations their specialty.

Among these Robert Weaver can be cited as perhaps the most conspicuous single example. The son of a postal clerk, Weaver had majored in economics at Harvard, getting his Ph.D. in 1934.

Brought into the Interior Department by Harold Ickes, Weaver became the informal head of a "Black Cabinet" of "race relations advisers," who were spread throughout the New Deal agencies. Later he served in successive government posts—in the Federal Housing Administration, the war production agencies, the United Nations Relief and Rehabilitation Administration, and the State Rent Commission in New York. In 1961 President Kennedy named him head of the Housing and Home Finance Agency. In urging the creation of a new Department of Urban Affairs, Kennedy planned to make Weaver, as head of the new department, the first Negro in the Cabinet.

These government appointees helped generate a sense of identification with the Democratic party among the younger Negroes, then in high school and college. An even more dramatic lift to Negro aspirations was provided by Eleanor Roosevelt, the first President's wife to demonstrate a warm, personal interest in Negroes as human beings. During the 1936 campaign the Negro Division of the Democratic party distributed a million photographs of Mrs. Roosevelt talking with Negro professors at Howard University.

Impressive as was each of these actions, they were less important than the truly revolutionary change that Roosevelt effected—bringing the Negro into the newly formed New Deal coalition of big city voters, which established the Democrats as the normal majority party in the country.

Before the New Deal the nation's workers had been divided by racial, religious and nationality differences. Native-stock Americans looked down with contempt upon immigrants; Protestants held themselves aloof from Catholics, whites from blacks.

To all these elements once so hostile to each other Roosevelt imparted a common sense of economic class consciousness. The depression had left them with mutual grievances —unemployment, foreclosed homes, pay cuts, lost savings in banks that had closed—and common hatreds of bankers and employers. Roosevelt also stirred in all of these voting elements new expectations of what the government would do for people.

From 1936 on, in every presidential election, the voting in all of our Northern cities would stratify sharply along economic lines. The lower the income in any neighborhood the heavier the Democratic vote. As one climbed the rungs of the economic ladder, Republican strength would rise proportionately.

Cementing the Negro into this coalition were three main appeals: his stake in govenment programs, his attachment to the big city machines, which in city after city came under Democratic control, and the newly formed CIO to which Negroes were admitted on the same basis as white workers.

For Negroes the CIO symbolized the most revolutionary change touched off by the New Deal. Since slave days white and Negro workers had looked on each other as hated economic rivals. During the Populist agitation in the South, Tom Watson had tried to unite the poor white and poor black farmers, but when this effort failed he turned to "nigger baiting." In the Northern industrial cities as well, the AFL unions had traditionally barred Negroes from membership and Negroes had responded by serving as strikebreakers.

Many Negro leaders had preached that perhaps the Negro's chief economic asset was his readiness to work when the white man might not want to. In his Atlanta speech Booker T. Washington reminded his audience that in the Negro the South had a willing servant who "without strikes and labor wars, tilled your fields, cleaned your forests, builded your railroads and cities . . ."

Similarly Marcus Garvey, in warning Negroes to "beware of white labor unions," had said, "It seems strange but the only convenient friend the Negro workers or laborers have in America at the present time is the white capitalist."

In the CIO unions, however, the Negro was at last able to find a basis of common interest with white persons of the same economic class. Whether white or black, workers on the same job would draw identical pay. The same seniority rules that governed hiring and layoffs for whites applied to Negroes.

Nor was it accidental that the determination to write a new page in labor history proved strongest in the "open shop" industries like steel, meat packing, rubber and automobiles. These were the industries in which sizable numbers of Negroes were already employed. In these industries racial antagonisms had to be suppressed if a successful union was to be formed.

The steel strike in 1919, for example, had been broken by the importation of nearly 30,000 Negro strikebreakers. Similarly, when the Amalgamated Meat Cutters and Butchers tried to organize the meat packing industry the employers set up a rival Negro union. The American Unity Labor Union declared, "This union does not believe in strikes. We believe all differences between laborers and capitalists can be arbitrated. Strike is our last motive, if any at all."

By contrast, relatively few Northern Negroes had been

able to break into crafts like carpentering and plumbing. These unions faced no necessity to admit Negroes into their membership since they could maintain a monopoly control of available jobs without changing their racial policies.

This difference between industrial and craft unions explains much of the wrangling during recent years over the exclusion of Negroes from union membership. The New Deal alliance of Negroes and organized labor was not produced by any evangelistic conversion to a belief in the rights of man. Common necessity—the need to unite against employers—was the shotgun that arranged the wedding.

Where this cementing sense of common economic interest existed the Negro-labor alliance has remained quite strong. Wherever this same interest was not present, as with the Railroad Brotherhoods and the building trades, this Negro-labor alliance has tended to pull apart.

The cementing ties of the New Deal also have been weakened as the New Deal supporters prospered and moved up into the middle class. Union loyalties became less intense or, with white-collar workers, might cease to exist. Also white trade unionists who would defend the Negro's right to work alongside of the white man on a basis of complete equality would violently oppose the Negro's moving into the same residential street.

In retrospect it would also seem clear that the strengthening of the unions under the New Deal would pose new problems for those Negroes who moved north in the 1950's and 1960's. By the 1960's the free labor market would leave open a much smaller share of employment oppor-

tunity than had prevailed forty years earlier; Negroes seeking employment would be barred by union restrictions from
many lines of work which had been open to all newcomers
in the 1920's.

These considerations, however, were not in the minds of
the Negroes during the first CIO years. The fact that Negro
workers were being accepted as equals with white unionists
fired the imaginations not only of the Negro masses but of
their leaders. Many of them, like Walter White, wrote and
talked of organized labor with evangelistic fervor as bearing
the promise of complete racial and economic emancipation.
Negro intellectuals, who had generally been pro-business
during the 1920's, swung and tied their hopes for the future
to the new Negro-labor-liberal alliance.

This exhilarating sense of being part of the majority
coalition was strengthened by the expansion of employment during World War II. Even after Hitler overran
France large numbers of Negroes still remained unemployed. But in 1942, after A. Philip Randolph had
pressured Roosevelt into creating the FEPC, or Fair Employment Practices Commission, the color line began to
give. Between 1940 and 1944 more than a million Negroes,
many fresh off the farms in the South, found new jobs in
industry.

Some were employed in nondefense jobs deserted by
white workers; other Negroes were admitted into the construction trades in government plants. Still others broke
into aircraft and other defense work. Roughly 250,000
Negroes migrated to the Pacific coast.

In four to five years, as Robert Weaver calculated, the

number of Negroes in skilled jobs doubled. Many entered industries in which few if any Negroes had worked before. Those few war years, in fact, brought more diversification of Negro occupations than had occurred in the seventy-five preceding years.

Most Loyal of Democrats

With the end of World War II the political conversion of the Negro was all but completed. From a strikebreaker during the 1920's he had been transformed into the most faithful of union members; from the stanchest of Republicans into the most loyal of Democrats.

In 1948, with the Dixiecrats bolting in the South, Negroes rallied behind Harry Truman with a heavier percentage of their vote than they had given Franklin Roosevelt. Four years later, when nearly every other element in the Democratic coalition was breaking for Eisenhower, Negroes racked up an even larger percentage for Adlai Stevenson than they had for Truman.

The selection of a Southerner, Senator John Sparkman of Alabama, as Stevenson's vice-presidential running mate irritated most Negro leaders. After the 1952 convention was over, Walter White wrote an article for *Look* magazine headlined "Win Our Vote or Lose," in which he argued that the Negro vote was still undecided and would be won over by the position taken by the candidates on civil rights during the campaign.

Actually there never was any indecision among Negro voters. Immediately after the conventions I started across the country interviewing voters on the election. The Negroes interviewed in Los Angeles during early August were as firm in their intention to vote Democratic as were those I talked with in Harlem two months later.

White's thesis of an independent Negro vote was being pushed as a bargaining argument in the hope that both Stevenson and Eisenhower would compete against each other with promises of civil rights action. But my own interviews indicated that the Negro's main attachment to the Democratic party was primarily economic. Civil rights exerted only a secondary appeal.

"I've been thinking of voting for Eisenhower," said one 22-year-old Negro in Detroit, "but every time I mention it my father and mother start talking of the terrible time they had in the depression. Listening to them makes you want to vote Democratic."

Asked how he felt about a Southerner being on the ticket as Vice-President, a Negro laborer in St. Louis replied, "That don't mean anything. I'm a working man. How can I vote anything but Democratic?"

The wife of a Pittsburgh redcap pointed out: "We've been able to buy our own home and move up out of the hill [a slum district] under the Democrats. Why would we want to change?"

The Democratic loyalty expressed in these interviews, it is worth noting, extended beyond the Negro's interest as a labor union member. The comments also showed a general gratitude for economic gains and a preference for heavier government spending.

"It's easier to earn a buck under the Democrats," said

one Los Angeles musician. "When the Republicans get in the money goes somewhere. The big fellows must hold onto it."

After Eisenhower sent troops into Little Rock a sizable number of Negroes did begin to think that the Republicans might push civil rights more energetically than the Democrats. In a 1957 survey, when Negroes were asked which party was best for them on civil rights, a majority picked the Republicans. But these same Negroes named the Democrats as "the best party for jobs" by a 3 and 4 to 1 margin.

The Roosevelt and postwar years also brought tightened Democratic control of the larger cities. In Chicago gratitude for the patronage which Thompson had extended remained so strong that the Second Ward did not give Roosevelt a majority until 1944, while William Dawson, the Negro boss, was not able to solidify his control until 1948.

In Philadelphia, even while giving Roosevelt two thirds of their vote, the predominantly Negro wards continued to turn in Republican majorities for mayors. Not until the Democrats swept City Hall in 1955 did this gap between local and presidential voting disappear.

In New York City the La Guardia administration gained strong support in the Negro areas. But after his defeat in 1945 the Democratic hold on the Negro vote solidified.

The high Democratic percentages being cast by the Negroes do not mean that they are politically satisfied. However, these heavy percentages do indicate that the bulk of Negroes remain emotionally committed to the Democratic party as the political vehicle through which they hope to advance their interests. Put another way, Negro discontents are not operating to drive the Negroes out of the Democratic party or to break free of the big city machines or out of the labor unions. These discontents are being used to bargain for a larger share within the Democratic coalition.

In short, for the Democratic coalition the political danger posed by the swelling Negro vote is not that Negroes will bolt to the Republicans. The threat is that Negro demands may drive white Democratic voters out of the coalition.

This, of course, has been one impact that Negro voting has had upon the white South. As long as the Negroes voted Republican nationally they could exert little political leverage upon the South. Only by moving into the Democratic party could they really bring to a climax their battle to rewrite the Booker T. Washington years.

That may seem like a strange statement to persons who think that political parties should attract voters who share much the same views or to those who have wondered how the Negroes and white Southerners could dwell together in the same political house.

But the distinctive nature of the American party system lies in precisely this ability to attract clashing political elements. Under our political system the essential function of the majority party is to serve as an arena in which the dominant issues of the period can be fought out.

Both the strengths and the weaknesses of our party system reflect its arena-like nature. On the constructive side, the fact that a party is in constant conflict within itself enables it to perform the enormously important role of national unification. The majority coalition, being concerned with its own survival, has a high stake in finding some solution for the conflicts that divide the coalition.

But these same pressures to hold together the coalition can also prove a tragic weakness. Strive as they do, the party leaders may be unable to bring about genuine reconciliation. At most the leaders may be capable only of stitching and mending, of patching and repairing, when a really new garment is needed.

When that happens the coalition drifts into stalemate and deadlock. Symbolic compromises may be arrived at but they settle nothing. Primarily these compromises buy time until the ceaseless processes of social and economic change across the nation can throw new weights into the political scales, making it possible perhaps to break the deadlock.

This, of course, has been the pattern that the Negro-South struggle has followed. In moving north, the Negroes re-entered political life, upsetting the old balance of the Booker T. Washington era. But it was not long before the white South, through its power in Congress, was able to deadlock the Democratic party on civil rights.

Even while this deadlock prevailed in Washington new political feelings were being churned up all across the country. What impact have these changes had upon the South? Upon the North? Are they bringing us closer to an end of the racial deadlock? Or is time only spreading ever wider the cancer of racial strife?

5

Battle for the South

A Dream Dying

At the time the incident was shrugged off as little more than another of "Cotton Ed" Smith's eccentricities. In Washington the senior senator from South Carolina had been known for odd antics like ringing the Senate elevator button in Morse Code fashion or greeting King George with a slap on the back and a "Howdy, Majesty."

Therefore not much importance was attached to the fact that at the 1936 Democratic convention in Philadelphia Cotton Ed stalked out when Marshall Shepard, a Negro minister who had broken with GOP boss William Vare, delivered a prayer. Cotton Ed returned but the following day when Chicago's Negro congressman, Arthur Mitchell, rose to speak, Smith and eight other South Carolinians made for the exits again.

In retrospect, Cotton Ed's demonstration proved to be the first of a series of convention bolts and voting revolts staged by Southerners in their battle with the Negroes and Northern "liberals" for control of the Democratic party.

This struggle had a relatively slow buildup. For a time the Democratic leaders left the Negro sitting in the waiting room rather than in the parlor of the party. Neither the 1932 nor the 1936 Democratic platform contained any mention of the Negro. Not until 1940, when Roosevelt made his third-term bid, was a specific Negro plank put into the platform.

Two other events were needed to bring the struggle for party control fully into the open—the Supreme Court's decision of April 3, 1944, opening the "white primary" to Negro voters in the South and the death of Franklin Roosevelt.

While the primaries were closed to him, the Negro's vote in the South was pretty meaningless. It could not be cast effectively in contests for governor, U.S. senator or members of Congress, all of which were settled in the primary. In opening the primary the Supreme Court did not oust a single Southern officeholder, but it changed the terms on which the South's political battling would be conducted in the future.

Roosevelt's death, the following year, removed another restraint against open political rebellion in the South. Many

Southern voters felt a deep personal gratitude to "that man in the White House" who had saved their homes or farms from foreclosure, had raised their wages, and had introduced social security and other benefits.

With his death these ties of loyalty were snapped. The battle for dominance in the Democratic party between the white Southerners and the Northern liberals could at last be fully joined.

The strategy of the Northern Democrats called for a bold political thrust into the South. With the end of World War II industrialization in the South quickened. To Walter White and the CIO labor leaders this seemed to provide an ideal opportunity to remake the South in the image of Northern liberalism.

They foresaw the expansion of industry producing a dramatic growth in trade-union membership. Simultaneously they reasoned that Negroes would come to vote in ever-increasing numbers. Allied with other white progressive elements, the Negro and organized labor would give liberalism in the South a revolutionary new strength.

The dream, in short, was to project into the South the New Deal union of white and black workers that had been forged in the North. But this dream had collapsed even before the Supreme Court ordered schools desegregated.

After the "white primary" was opened, Negro registration in the eleven Southern states quadrupled quickly, jumping to over a million registrants by 1952. The first effects of this increased Negro voting, however, were to intensify an even heavier outpouring of anti-Negro white voters. By 1950 as well, although $6 million had been spent, the CIO found itself forced to all but abandon its drive to unionize Southern industry.

The basic error in judgment of the Northern liberals lay in their assumption that industrialization in the South would produce the same political pattern as it had in the North. Actually the dominant trends of economic change were operating to make the South more conservative rather than more liberal politically.

During those years roughly a fourth of the nation's total expenditures on new factories were going into the South. Decisions on locating these investments were being made by businessmen, not labor leaders, and it was for the favor of business that Southerners competed not only with liberal tax allowances but also with generous gifts of new factory sites.

This expansion of industry also generated the rise of new middle-class elements—lawyers, doctors, clerks, engineers —who identified the South's economic future with the interests of business. It was this new middle class that spearheaded the drive that swept four Southern states for Dwight D. Eisenhower in 1952.

The heightened racial conflict that followed the Supreme Court's desegregation decision pushed the dream of a liberal labor-Negro coalition even further from realization.

Union members formed a sizable proportion of the membership of the White Citizens' Councils which were formed to fight the Court's decision. The activities of these Citizens' Councils also weakened the small number of "liberals" in the South. Traditionally these liberals had occupied the middle ground between the Negroes and the hostile white community. But as racial feelings polarized, this middle ground was cut away.

During 1955 and 1956 the Southern Regional Council recorded more than a hundred incidents of violence, intimidation or reprisal in opposition to the Supreme Court's decision.

Negro churches and homes were bombed; robed nightriders fired shots into Negro homes at night; acid was thrown on Negro-owned cars; many Negroes were beaten; some were killed. The anger of Negroes was inflamed further by the rioting that accompanied the expulsion of Autherine Lucy from the University of Alabama and by the murder of Emmett Till, a 14-year-old Negro from Chicago, who, while visiting relatives in Mississippi, allegedly whistled at the wife of a white storekeeper.

In the face of this violence white liberals found it increasingly difficult to speak out publicly in favor of the Negro. Negroes, on the other hand, felt more and more that they had to strike back, even if it meant fighting alone.

In Houston, Texas, for example, a loose sort of understanding existed under which Negroes joined with labor unions and other "progressive" groups in supporting "liberal" candidates. When the 1956 campaign for the school board started, the liberal leaders wanted to avoid the segregation issue, believing that raising it meant certain defeat. When this view was presented to Carter Wesley, who publishes a string of Negro newspapers in the Houston area, he insisted the segregation question be met head on. Declaring "it's time to stand up and be counted" Wesley demanded the coalition run a Negro as one of its candidates. When the coalition refused, a Negro entered the race independently. He was defeated, along with the entire liberal slate.

"We knew we couldn't win without liberal support," explained Wesley, "but we showed them they could not win without us either."

The anger that had been building up among Negroes exploded dramatically in the 1956 presidential election. In 1952, in 86 cities studied, Eisenhower had drawn roughly a quarter of the vote in predominantly Negro wards and precincts. These same wards and precincts jumped their vote for him by 11 percentage points in 1956.

Ordinarily a shift of 5 percentage points in a presidential election will make the difference between a close contest and a landslide. The extent of this Negro break was all the more startling, considering the habitual party loyalty of the Negro voter. From 1940 through 1952 the Negroes had given each successive Democratic candidate for President a higher percentage of their vote than in the preceding election.

Significantly, the swing to Eisenhower was far heavier among Southern than among Northern Negroes. Both shared the same resentment against racial violence and against being taken for granted by the Democratic party. In the North, however, much of this anger was deflected by the hold of the big city machines, labor unions and the New

Deal's economic appeal. In the South there were no coalition interests to stem the anger.

While Eisenhower gained 8 percentage points among Northern Negroes he more than doubled his vote among Southern Negroes. Some of these shifts were astonishing.

The all-Negro Fifth Ward in Greensboro, N.C., had given Eisenhower only 5 percent of its vote in 1952. In 1956 it went to 66 percent.

Six Negro precincts in Richmond, Va., which had voted 15 percent for Eisenhower in 1952, gave him 74 percent in 1956.

At the time not too much significance was attached to this Negro voting break. But in the light of what has happened since, the 1956 election seems to have marked a historic political shift on the part of the Southern Negro. Sometime during those two violent years of 1955 and 1956—perhaps it was with the Montgomery bus boycott—the Southern Negro turned his back on the liberal dream of a coalition with Southern labor and struck out on his own into a new orbit of political conflict.

The New Urban Arena

Spurring this new political turn was the urbanization of the South. In the decade between 1950 and 1960 a record number of Southern whites and Negroes left the land. These were the years in which cotton planting was being mechanized. Often the labor needs of a plantation were cut to a tenth of what they had been before. As late as 1952 the Green Suttle plantation outside of Selma had been worked by 48 Negro families. At the time of the march to Montgomery, only three Negroes were left on the land.

While many whites and Negroes moved north, others drifted into the larger towns and cities in the South. With them they brought their own racial prejudices. Almost automatically they turned the cities into a battleground over whether the racial attitudes of the rural South would be transferred to the cities.

Sharpening this conflict was the fact that most state legislatures tended to reflect rural racial views; on the other hand, it was easier for the Negroes to press for federal court action in the cities.

In the ensuing struggle the Negroes quickly found that their natural political allies were not the Democratic-voting white workers but the better-income elements, who leaned Republican in presidential voting.

Little Rock provided a dramatic illustration of this alignment. After Gov. Orval Faubus blocked the entrance of nine Negro children to Central High School, the Little Rock school board became the center of intense conflict. In three years, from 1957 to 1960, five elections took place which affected the membership of the school board.

In all five elections, as can been seen in Table III, the predominantly Negro precincts voted along with the upper-income white neighborhoods, such as Pulaski Heights. The heaviest segregationist vote was concentrated in the lower-income white areas, near the Central High School.

The decisive break came in the May, 1958, election, when despite two television appeals by Governor Faubus, three segregationists were eliminated from the school board, clearing the way for reopening Little Rock schools in late

TABLE III.   *School Issue Voting in Little Rock*

| | % Favoring Segregationist View | | | | |
	Nov. 1957	Dec. 1958	May 1959	Dec. 1959	Nov. 1960
Low Income Whites	60	67	58	49	36
Upper Income Whites	33	29	22	16	16
Negro*	28	27	26	19	22
Whole City	48	50	44	31	27

* The Negro precincts are not entirely Negro in population.

August of 1959. In the 1960 election, when Governor Faubus sought power to close the schools again, even segregationist precincts turned the proposal down.

The balloting in 1960 also included a referendum proposal for a state-wide minimum wage. On this economic issue, as will be seen in Table IV, the Negroes and lower-income whites voted together, even while being far apart on the school closing proposal.

These two tables of Little Rock voting can be looked on as a capsule picture of Southern voting today. On economic issues some sense of common interest binds white and Negro workers. But on racial issues the better-income elements and Negroes tend to be closest together.

In short, the pattern reflects no unified political coalition as has existed in the Northern states under which the Negro's racial and economic interests were dovetailed with those of white voters of the same economic class. In the South the prevailing pattern has been one of makeshift alignments from one contest to another.

TABLE IV.   *Economics vs. Race, Little Rock 1960*

	% against minimum wage	% for school closing	% for Nixon
Negro	47	22	42
Low Income White	48	36	31
Upper Income White	79	16	55

The city of Atlanta provides another made-to-order illustration of the sharp polarization of voting that is taking place in many Southern cities on racial issues. Like Caesar's Gaul, Atlanta is divided into three parts, each displaying astonishingly rigid racial attitudes. Nor has doubling the city's population changed this stratification.

On "the north side" live the relatively well-to-do, largely business-oriented whites. Many are white-collar employees or managers of regional distribution centers and Northern branch plants. On this north side are found most wealthy and influential Atlantans, the "liberals," and nearly all Northerners who have come south.

South-side Atlanta also is almost entirely white, but in the local vernacular is "redneck country." The residents are mainly factory workers or elderly people living on small pensions. In many ways they are still "country boys" wearing the shoes of the big city as if their feet hurt them.

Bond issues for improving municipal services are likely to draw only a third of the vote among south-siders, who not only dislike paying taxes but have low expectations as to the level of services a government should furnish its citizenry.

While most of the newer homes on the north side are modern, such houses do not sell well in the south side. There the preference runs to homes of the more conventional old South type.

South-siders tend also to be dry and Baptist. There are fewer liquor stores per capita in South Atlanta than in the north side. This allocation is attributed to an understanding between some ministers and the whiskey dealers. The stores that do exist make more money, of course.

Funneled between the two white ends of Atlanta stretches the expanding black belt of more than 180,000 Negroes. For a time nearly all of the Negroes were bottled up in the center of town, with millionaires living next to slums. Then a new suburban Negro development was opened on the west side with homes ranging from $10,000 to $100,000.

As the Negro population expands it tends to move southward rather than northward—a detail which helps preserve the alliance of Negroes and upper-income whites.

But perhaps the most remarkable feature about this three-way stratification of Atlanta is how little it has changed despite the city's spectacular growth. As the city's population has expanded, each of the three areas has simply attracted more of its own kind.

Between 1957 and 1961 the total vote cast in the elections for mayor rose by more than half — from 65,287 to 100,404. Still the voting alignment of the three sections remained almost constant. In both elections the losing candidate was Lester Maddox, a militant segregationist who, when the 1964 civil rights law went into effect, sold out his restaurant rather than serve Negroes. In both of his races for mayor Maddox drew a third of Atlanta's vote. The vote for his opponents — former Mayor William Hartsfield in 1957 and Ivan Allen in 1961 — varied only slightly in all three sections of the city (see Table V).

This showcase picture of Atlanta's voting also illustrates the importance of Negro suffrage in maintaining an equitably balanced community racially. If, during recent years, Atlanta's Negroes had been denied the right to vote, the south side white population would have grown sufficiently to gain

TABLE V. *A Racial Profile: Voting in Atlanta*

	For Mayor Hartsfield	For Ivan Allen
	Percentage	
	1957	1961
Negro Precincts	90	94
White North Side	74	76
White South Side	38	40
Whole City	63.7	64

political control of the city. Atlanta might have become another Birmingham.

In both Atlanta and Birmingham Negroes comprise close to 40 percent of the population. But where Atlanta's Negroes cast about a fourth of the city's vote, Birmingham's Negroes account for only about 8 percent of the city's registration. Birmingham also suffers from the fact that much of its well-to-do citizenry lives in suburbs and has no say in how the city is run.

In other Southern cities Negro leaders have adopted a deliberate strategy of shifting from party to party simply to demonstrate their voting strength and increase their bargaining power. Negro registration in Richmond, Va., for example, has been pushed to 14,000, nearly a fourth of the 1964 city total.

When Senator Harry F. Byrd ran for re-election in 1958, the Negro precincts in Richmond voted 90 percent against him. Two years later they gave Kennedy 63 percent of their vote. In the 1962 Congressional elections they shifted parties once more, voting 73 percent for the Republican candidate for Congress, bringing him within 340 votes of victory. Again in 1963 when Richmond elected two Republicans to the General Assembly for the first time in many years the balance of victory was supplied by the Negro vote. Goldwater, though, drew only 1% of the vote in the heaviest Negro precincts.

In Memphis, Russell Sugarmon, Jr., one of the more militant Negro leaders, has pursued the tactic of running Negro candidates for local offices to stimulate Negro political interest. Between 1959 and 1963 Negro registration in Memphis rose from 50,000 to 69,000, roughly a third of the total registration in the city, probably the highest Negro-to-white voting proportion in the South. In 1962 and 1964 Negroes provided the votes that defeated Robert James, a Goldwater conservative, for Congress.

Through the whole South the gains in Negro registration have not been so spectacular as Negro leaders had hoped. Encouraged by the quick rise in Negro registration when the white primary was opened, NAACP leaders forecast that 3 million Negroes would be registered in the South by 1956. Actually for 1956 the Southern Regional Council estimated that 1,230,000 Negroes were registered. By 1963 Negro registration had risen to 1,579,081, which was less than 30 percent of all Negroes of voting age in the South, compared with 60 percent among Southern whites of voting age. By November, 1964, the Southern Regional Council put the Negro registration at 2,174,000 or 43 percent of the eligible Negroes.

In a closely fought contest this Negro vote can be decisive. Both North Carolina and South Carolina were probably held in the Democratic column for John Kennedy in 1960 by the Negro vote. In 1964 four of the six Southern states which Johnson carried were won by margins less than the vote cast by Negroes. The Negroes alone were not responsible for the Democratic victories in these states. In all of them Goldwater lost Eisenhower-Nixon supporters among white voters as well. Still, the plurality of nearly 1,500,000 votes which Southern Negroes are estimated (by the Southern Regional Council) to have given Johnson has certainly made them a new political force in the South.

With the new Voting Rights Law another million or more Negro voters may be added to the registration rolls. This seems likely to moderate Southern violence against Negroes and has also sparked anew hopes for a Negro-labor-liberal coalition in the South that would be allied with a similar coalition in the North.

But whether political conditions will favor such an alliance remains doubtful.

At least two conflicting currents should be noted. First, some of the more uncompromising Negroes — generally the younger SNCC militants who started the whole sit-in movement in the South — oppose any political tie-in with whites. They have argued for the creation of an independent Negro party in the South, modeled after the Mississippi Freedom Party. The Mississippi Freedom demonstrations at the Democratic presidential convention in Atlantic City were the first public expression of determination by some Southern Negroes to fight it out alone, without "liberal" white allies.

Second, even if other Negro leaders decide they need white support, there is no certainty that the most effective allies will be found among liberals and labor unions. As long as the desegregation war rages, who controls City Hall may be as important for the Southern Negro as who sits in the White House. Who runs the city will influence, if not determine, the quality of schools and housing that Negroes get; how effective negotiations to open job opportunities prove; how the police force is handled during demonstrations — by a Bull Connor or someone else.

In state elections as well Negroes are likely to find more common interest in joining with urban voters, who lean Republican in national voting, against the more Democratic but anti-Negro rural areas. About half the Southern Negro vote is now concentrated in the major cities. Reapportionment is undercutting the old rural dominance in state legislatures, which probably will bring new political alignments. Until these alignments are set the Negro leaders would be unwise to freeze their political support.

In some states the Negroes may become a Republican bulwark.

Little Rock's predominantly Negro precincts gave Goldwater only 14 percent of their vote but went 80 percent for Winthrop Rockefeller in his 1964 race against Orville Faubus.

Still another uncertainty will be the impact of the fair employment provisions of the Civil Rights Law. The act charges employers with the responsibility for ending discrim-

ination in employment, which means that they are likely to
be leading the fight for compliance, while resistance to the
law may come primarily from the Southern labor unions.

For some years to come, in short, the interests of the
Southern Negro may not fit into the traditional New Deal
slots. His shrewdest political strategy may continue to be
one of free-wheeling flexibility between both parties and
candidates.

Possibly in time a Negro-labor coalition may take hold in
the South; but there is also a contrary prospect that the militancy of the Southern Negroes could weaken the New Deal
coalition in the North.

The Militancy of Martin King

Viewed against this backdrop it is not surprising that a
new, more volatile Negro leadership should emerge in the
South. Being part of no coalition, the Southern Negro has
been free of many of the restraints that tie down Negroes
in the North. But in the South the Negro has been fighting for a wholly new definition of his status, a definition
that must be written quickly before the urbanizing South
rigidifies.

A strategy of dragging one's rights through successive
courts would waste time that the Southern Negro does not
have. Also these changes must be won simultaneously on
many points, not alone on schools but on buses, lunch count-
ers, jobs — across the whole of living.

Why Martin Luther King, Jr., emerged as the symbolic
leader of this struggle may be mere chance. Many of the
demonstrations, such as the first sit-ins in Greensboro, were
spontaneous actions begun by Negro collegians. Also, different Negro groups have competed with one another in

their readiness to go to jail. Still, a "movement" of this nature usually requires a popular hero to serve as the symbolic if not the actual leader. Whoever emerged as the leader probably would have possessed much the same characteristics as King has, posing the same revolutionary contrast with Booker T. Washington in the Negro's makeup and status.

Three qualities stand out when King is compared with previous Negro leaders:

First, he is surprisingly young. He was only twenty-six years old, out of graduate school only a year, when the leadership of the Montgomery bus boycott was thrust upon him. He was so new to Montgomery that he had never cast a vote in the city and had had little time to adjust to what Negroes there were accustomed to doing—and not doing.

Second, his personal upbringing had given him a totally different self-image of the Negro from that held by earlier racial leaders. Washington's image of the Negro was born of slavery; that of Du Bois out of intellectual loneliness, Abbott's out of self-hatred, Garvey's out of caste bitterness. King's thinking is completely the product of middle-class stability and confidence.

Third, there is the enormously important fact that he grew up in a strongly father-centered family. Neither Frederick Douglass nor Booker T. Washington knew who his father was; when Du Bois was young his father "faded out of the picture" and Will was raised by his mother; Garvey's father lost the property he had owned by the time Marcus grew up.

In many ways the real story of young Martin King is the

story of his father Martin Luther, Sr. and of his father's generation. They had to test and select the traits of character that would prove enduring; they had to amass the economic resources that would shelter dignity and courage; they had to live with one another on terms of self-respect that their children could take for granted.

The second of ten children, Martin Luther King, Sr., was born on December 19, 1899, in rural Stockbridge, about twenty miles from Atlanta on the way to Macon. His father, James Albert King, was part Irish and part Negro, a none-too-successful sharecropper who went from one season's debt to the next. Usually when his cotton was sold his share would just about pay for the "furnishings" the landlord had provided during the past year. When he wasn't toiling in the fields he was drinking.

One Saturday night Papa came home and began to abuse and beat his wife. Martin grabbed his father, hurled him to the ground, and was choking him when his mother pulled him away.

Remembering the Stockbridge days, Martin Sr. set out to be the kind of father he had never had. He made himself the center of responsibility in the house. Each of his four children was given a weekly allowance large enough so they could drop one coin in the church collection plates and another in the coin bank, with something extra for an ice-cream cone or soda.

The elder Reverend Mr. King is a proud man. He would not permit any of his children to work for white families, fearing it might habituate the children to subservience. Nor would he ride the segregated buses of Atlanta.

Martin Jr. recalls one incident that occurred when he was six years old. His father had taken him to a shoe store in the main part of Atlanta. They sat down in the front of the store while waiting to be served. When the young white clerk appeared he said, "I'll be happy to wait on you, if you'll just move back there to those seats in the rear."

"There's nothing wrong with these seats," the elder King said, bristling.

"Sorry," insisted the clerk, "but you'll have to go back there."

"We'll either buy shoes sitting right here or we won't buy your shoes at all," snorted the father. There was a brief, awkward pause. Then father and son stalked out.

The Atlanta Negro community had learned to fight for its rights. Walter White, then an Atlanta resident, tells the story of how Atlanta Negroes organized in 1916 to defeat a school bond issue which was intended to improve white but not Negro schools. Under the city charter bond issues had to be approved by two thirds of the registered voters.

A house-to-house drive was organized to get Negroes to pay their poll tax and register. When the bond issue was defeated, the city officials agreed to give the Negroes a high school in return for their support of a second bond issue.

During the bond issue battle the Atlanta *Georgian* was bitter in its attacks on the Negroes. The Reverend Adam D. Williams of Ebenezer Baptist Church organized a boycott of the paper. It was Williams' daughter whom Martin King, Sr., married, later succeeding Williams as pastor of the Ebenezer Church.

Martin Sr. has done his own share of battling for Negro

rights. He led the fight to equalize teachers' salaries in Atlanta and joined in the battle to desegregate the elevators in the courthouse. This readiness to assert his rights has remained characteristic of the man. On New Year's Day of 1961 while waiting for young Martin to come to address the church, the elder King mounted the pulpit and delivered an extemperaneous scolding.

"We all got a bundle of new rights this year," he began. "I've been looking to see how many of you are using these new rights. I don't see many of you in the lunch room in Rich's Department Store. I don't see you riding up front in the buses. I don't see you in the libraries.

"I know it costs money to eat uptown," he went on. "But this is freedom money. Everybody ought to put some freedom money in his budget. Let's make that a New Year's resolution.

"And another thing, when you go to Rich's to eat," he concluded, "don't bunch—scatter."

Both the Ebenezer Baptist Church and the house where young Martin was born in 1929 stand on Auburn Avenue, perhaps the proudest Negro street in the United States. Only seventeen blocks long, Auburn Avenue is a remarkable concentration of Negro enterprise and wealth. Well over $100 million in financial resources are represented in the Negro institutions that stand on the street. The yellow brick Atlanta Life Insurance Company has assets of $60 million, the Citizens Trust Company has deposits of $11.3 million.

Most of the members of the Ebenezer Baptist Church are workers, skilled, semiskilled and unskilled. But the congregation also includes office employees and teachers, a few doctors and lawyers, and some of Atlanta's most influential Negroes—C. A. Scott, the publisher of the Atlanta *Daily World,* and E. B. Blayton, the wealthy executive president of the Mutual Federal Savings & Loan whose assets total $10 million.

In recent years psychologists have contended that segregation by itself breeds an innate sense of inferiority. Yet certainly young Martin King did not come out of Auburn Avenue feeling shame or fear. To the contrary, his walk seems always to have been buoyed up by a springy sense of Negro accomplishment.

The high school he went to was one to which the "best" Negro families sent their children. Many of his classmates went on with him to Morehouse College, one of the few Southern colleges financed and run by Negroes. From Morehouse he continued his education for the ministry at Crozer Seminary in Pennsylvania and at Boston University, where he got his Ph.D.

His, in short, was a sheltered life in childhood and his youthful years, sheltered much as were many white youths of his age, by a strong family and comfortable economic means.

The contrast with Booker T. Washington is instructive. As a slave Washington had learned all the things a Negro in the South couldn't do, but Martin King was never really educated in what Langston Hughes once termed "the white man's ways."

As a child Martin suffered some insults because of his color. Once, while riding a bus from Macon to Atlanta, he was ordered to give up his seat to a white passenger and had to stand for ninety miles. His one visit to a segregated movie house in downtown Atlanta "was so obnoxious," he recalled, "that I could not enjoy the picture." He never went to a segregated movie house again.

Still Martin never was forced to lower his ambitions because of his color. While at college, when asked what he wanted to do when he grew up, he talked dreamily of owning a yacht. This acceptance of equality inside their own minds is perhaps the crucial factor that distinguishes the younger Southern Negroes from those of the past. Leslie Dunbar of the Southern Regional Council has pointed out that nearly all the Negro sit-ins were started in communities where a group of Negro colleges were situated close to each other. It has been the educated Negro who has taken the lead in voicing his dissatisfaction with the old status of the Negro.

In the end the white South will have to come to terms with how the Negro sees himself.

Every act of "nonviolence" by Negroes — the eagerness with which Negro high school students filled the jails in Birmingham, and defied Sheriff Jim Clark in Selma — has flashed into the minds of the South a facsimile image of a new kind of Negro.

The more extreme segregationists have tried to reject this new image, but their failure only emphasizes that more and more of the white South is coming to accept this new sense of Negro self-respect.

In fighting back the Negro is rewriting Southern history. After the Civil War the newly emancipated Negro was still superstitious, illiterate, credulous. Nor could he stand up long before the white man's anger.

Back in 1890 the Negroes of Meriwether Township,

92 WHITE AND BLACK

South Carolina, organized two militia companies to defend their rights. But the companies were disbanded after a few terrorist raids by "Red Shirt" vigilantes, led by Ben Tillman's brother, and threats by the plantation landlords to employ no Negro who belonged to the militia.

In Montgomery, though, the Negroes were able to operate a bus boycott for a full year. At Tuskegee, the effort to gerrymander Negroes out of their voting rights was fought with an economic boycott that lasted for several years. In Orangeburg, S.C., an economic war of nerves between whites and Negroes has been going on since 1955.

Much of this new Negro staying power reflects, of course, the shift from a rural to an urban society, which has nourished a securely rooted urban middle class. To carry through the Montgomery boycott leaflets had to be mimeographed and circulated; a car pool had to be organized to ease the strains of walking; a Negro lawyer had to be on hand to defend the boycotters who were arrested and to press the court action which finally declared segregated seating on buses unconstitutional.

None of these middle-class measures would have been available to Negroes in the sharecropper countryside.

When sit-in demonstrators were jailed, the local Negro communities had the financial resources to pay bail and legal costs and to carry through shopping boycotts that were effective. Again, the tactics of selective buying and economic boycott could not even have been dreamed of by croppers, who rarely saw any cash, were always in debt to their landlords, and were lucky if, when the cotton was sold, there was any money left over and coming to them.

In this testing of his stamina the Negro has suffered some defeats. In 1955 the NAACP confidently ordered its local chapters in Mississippi to file suits for the desegregation of schools. When fifty-three Negroes in Yazoo City signed a court petition, the local Citizens' Council bought a full-page advertisement listing the names and adresses of the signers. Reprisals quickly thinned the petition signers until only two were left.

But other Negroes, like Aaron Henry, who headed the Mississippi Freedom Party's delegation to the 1964 Democratic convention, did not leave the state. When the pharmacy that Henry owned in Clarksdale was bombed, he put two documents on display behind the smashed store windows — the Declaration of Independence and the Emancipation Proclamation.

Still, any weighing of the strength of the forces in conflict leaves no possible conclusion other than that the Southern Negro can look for only a partial victory, if left to battle on his own. His gains, moreover, are bound to fall unevenly, being most sparse in the least urbanized areas of the Deep South, where the Negro now exerts the least bargaining power and suffers the worst treatment. The same lack of bargaining strength which explains why his present status is so low deprives him of the ability to change those conditions. Where the Negro can show more muscle he will be able to assert more of his rights.

What Southern Negroes can do on their own, however, constitutes only part of the struggle. Significant changes have taken place in the attitudes of many white Southerners toward desegregation. Where are these changes moving the white South?

6

The Second Civil War

The South Mobilizes

On the day the Supreme Court declared segregation unconstitutional the Savannah, Ga., chapter of Rotary was holding a luncheon meeting. When a news flash of the Court's decision was read to the group there was a burst of applause.

Other newspaper clippings at the time indicated at least a grudging acceptance by many Southerners of the Court's decision when it first was announced. In Greensboro, N.C., the school board voted 6 to 1 to admit Negroes into white schools. Virginia's state superintendent of public instruction, when asked for comment, replied, "There will be no defiance of the Supreme Court as far as I'm concerned." The first public reaction of Price Daniel, then in the U.S.

94

Senate and later to be governor of Texas was "Let us accept the law and try to live with the gradual changes it must surely bring."

But it wasn't long before items like these vanished from the newspapers. After the Court's decision I began making regular swings through the South, interviewing typical Southerners. Each successive trip revealed a further hardening of resistance toward desegregation, with racial feelings more tense, more hostile than on the previous trip.

By early 1957, six months before Little Rock, I was writing that an armed clash between the federal and the state government was coming.

No action was more repugnant to President Dwight Eisenhower than the use of federal troops to enforce the Court's decision. Pressed for his views at news conferences, he persistently avoided any comment that white Southerners might consider hostile. He shied away from saying in so many words that the Court's decision was morally right. At one press session he warned, "If you try to go too far, too fast, you're making a mistake." At another news conference he maintained, "You cannot change people's thinking by laws."

Such comments suggest that Eisenhower had anything but a soldier's view of what was happening in the South. He seemed to regard the struggle of public opinion raging there as primarily a conflict of people with extremely strong convictions and whose minds could be altered only slowly as they argued among themselves.

Actually the struggle of public opinion being waged in

the South was much like that of a nation preparing for
war. It was not a peaceful debate between individual Southerners but a mobilization of the forces of warlike conformity, for warlike resistance against the federal government.

The Supreme Court, in implementing its 1954 decision,
had tried to develop a "divide and integrate" strategy.
By empowering each federal district court to adjust the pace
of desegregation to local conditions, the nine justices in
Washington apparently hoped to split the solidarity of the
South.

Those states or even parts of a state with the fewest
Negroes were expected to mix colored and white children
with the least difficulty. School districts with high proportions of Negroes in relation to whites were to be allowed
more drag in compliance.

But the segregationists quickly put their own counter-
strategy into action. To prevent the South from being
chipped off piece by piece, totalitarian controls were instituted. State constitutions were amended to authorize shut-
ting down public schools rather than permit desegregation.
Laws were passed providing for the denial of state school
funds to any community that broke out of the segregation
mold. The school superintendent in Norfolk, Va., had declared his readiness to abide by the Court's decision as had
the Arlington school board. But both communities were
blocked from integrating by the sovereign state of Virginia.

Simultaneously moderate opinion in the South was virtually silenced. In the immediate months after the Supreme
Court's decision many Southerners I interviewed were un-

sure which way to turn. Few welcomed the Court's verdict but many were troubled by the thought of defying so venerable an institution as the Supreme Court. Others felt that segregation was fundamentally unchristian and immoral.

But soon, where these doubts persisted, their expression came to be limited to the privacy of small groups or to one's own conscience. Outwardly at least an almost monolithic unity of opposition to desegregation was imposed. Some of the actions taken to enforce this conformity seemed silly, such as the cancellation of a soapbox derby in Augusta, Ga., because two Negro lads entered the contest with eighty white boys.

But other actions cut with a jagged edge. In Florence, S.C., John H. O'Dowd had opened his editorial page to what he thought of as a free discussion for both sides of the desegregation issue. But the abuse visited on him and his staff—their tires were slashed and their cars were chased at night—forced him to discontinue the arguments. Eventually he went north.

Other editors who favored gradual desegregation learned to keep their views to themselves. One Alabama editor, in refusing an invitation to speak off the record before a small pro-integration group, explained, "I must keep quiet now if I am to be able to exert any influence in the future."

Much of this intimidation, it should be noted, was targeted not at Negroes but at white persons. A few typical incidents might be cited:

In Montgomery's courthouse square two effigies were hanged, one representing a Negro labeled "NAACP," the other a white man tagged "I talked for integration."

At Opelika, Ala., robed Klansmen burned a cross in front of the home of a white Baptist minister who had admitted a Negro high school group into his church to hear a presentation of the *Messiah*.

For lunching with a Negro nurse in the course of a business day a Florida health officer was fired from her job.

Certainly in the White House these developments were not understood. When the Supreme Court's decision first was announced President Eisenhower told the Commissioners of the District of Columbia to desegregate the local schools as an example to the nation. But in the months that followed he avoided saying or doing anything that might influence public opinion in the South.

Yet the lack of effective opposition to the segregationists was changing the nature of Southern resistance to the Court. At first most Southerners looked upon opposition to desegregation as mainly a delaying action. They conceded that the Court's decree would have to be complied with eventually, but hoped that resistance would slow the pace of change.

By March of 1956, though, a "manifesto" signed by ninety-six Southern members of Congress publicly challenged the Supreme Court's constitutional right to make its decision and pledged to use "all lawful means" to reverse the verdict. Throughout the South my interviews showed a rising belief that the Court could be defied completely and the decision nullified.

By then the basic fact was that the pro-integration forces, routed and driven underground, no longer had even the semblance of any plan to obtain enforcement. The original

Court strategy had been trampled into the dirt; nor had any new strategy of enforcement been devised.

In his published diary E. Frederic Morrow, who was serving as the "first Negro assistant to a President," tells of repeated frustrations in trying to get White House action. Convinced of Eisenhower's "moral honesty" on the issue, Morrow still complains that he never could determine what was going on in the minds of the President and his more intimate advisers.

Still Morrow's account should not be read too literally. Every President, in assembling his staff, is guided by two prime considerations: the abilities of the individuals selected and the political pressures that the President is sensitive to and wants to be reminded of, even if he doesn't heed them.

Inside the Eisenhower White House the viewpoint of the more conservative Republicans was faithfully articulated by Jack Martin who had served Senator Robert Taft as administrative assistant. The liaison men dealing with Congress—General Wilton Persons and Gerry Morgan—could be counted on to transmit the "go slow" cautionings of key members of the Senate and House. There were also any number of other presidential aides who could relay telephone calls from Southern governors complaining that they had their racial hands full without White House "interference."

But the voice of the Negro rarely was plugged into the buzzer system on Eisenhower's desk. Negro voters, of course, had not contributed to Eisenhower's 1952 landslide; also some White House officials seem to have been irritated by the fact that public opinion polls showed only slight Republican gains among Negroes, despite Eisenhower's actions in desegregating the District of Columbia and other federal installations such as the Charleston, S.C., navy yard. At staff conferences arguments for further actions would prompt the retort that doing things for Negroes brought the Republicans no political gains.

Beyond this it also seems clear that no one in the White House (or outside of it) really knew what to do about Southern defiance. The only specific suggestions made to Morrow were for a White House meeting with key Negro leaders or that the President issue "a strong ringing statement deploring the breakdown of law and order in the South."

Both suggestions could be easily shrugged off by White House aides as "mere words." If the discussion went further to envision actual intervention, then the imaginations of White House aides would go to work pointing out the many difficulties.

One key presidential aide recalls one such conference at which questions like these were fired back at anyone suggesting federal action:

Could a mob be handled merely by clapping the leaders in jail or simply using U.S. marshals? Or would troops have to be called in?

Did the Attorney General have a large enough staff to handle all the violations taking place?

What if bloody race riots broke out in the South?

What if they spread to the North?

How deeply involved would the government become?

In summing up the situation at the time this White House aide recalled, "We were in a vacuum. Nothing like this defiance of a Court order had happened before. There was no real pressure in the country for any specific action."

There were, in truth, no precedents to guide the Administration, nor sufficient conviction to try something new.

By the spring of 1957 the segregationists, emboldened by the lack of opposition to their efforts, had come to believe that nullification of the Supreme Court's decision was in sight. They interpreted statements from the White House as indicating that the President had no heart for a showdown struggle on enforcement. Some Southern governors prepared to use their own police powers to block compliance with the Court's decree.

As late as July Eisenhower still was assuring his press conference, "I can't imagine any set of circumstances that would ever induce me to send federal troops into an area to enforce the orders of a federal court."

But by September 24 Governor Orval Faubus had left the President no other choice—either use troops or see the Court decision nullified.

The Turning Point

For Southern Negroes, the intervention at Little Rock was a decisive turning point, marking the conception of a new strategy of militancy. Until President Eisenhower acted there was no assurance that the power of the federal government would be used to uphold the Court. But at Little Rock the precedent was set. From then on Negroes could always hope for federal intervention if rioting and violence got out of hand.

For white Southerners, though, the turning point in the desegregation war came more than a year later, with the actual closing of the public schools in Little Rock and Norfolk.

Quite abruptly a new choice confronted the South. The question no longer was whether schools should or should not be integrated, whether the Supreme Court's orders could be successfully defied. The choice now was which was better—to accept a few Negroes on a token basis or to close the public schools?

Early in 1960 I went through much of the South asking just that question. Two of every three persons interviewed in ten Southern cities responded, "Better keep the schools open, even with a few Negroes in them."

Two years earlier a survey in many of these same cities had shown that only one fourth of the people favored integration.

The switch in public sentiment did not reflect any basic change of heart toward desegregation. The new readiness to accept token integration was simply a matter of taking the lesser of two evils.

Also, the change remained primarily an urban one. In rural counties the overwhelming majority of persons interviewed still held to the view "close the schools rather than have any mixing."

Significantly, token integration drew its heaviest support in those cities in which public schools had been closed and private schools were tried and abandoned.

In Norfolk an average of only one person in twelve preferred the schools shut rather than mixed. The predominant feeling was one of relief that the public schools were open again.

An electrician's wife recalled, "Private schools cost too much and weren't very good. Classes were held in church. The children had to sit on little kindergarten chairs. We all felt so disorganized."

A telephone mechanic's wife recalled, "My husband was very much against having Negroes in schools until he saw kids walking the streets." The wife of a city policeman, whose 14-year-old daughter attended Norview High, said, "I was more satisfied with segregated schools but this is better than closed schools."

Mixing the children had brought no trouble.

One 14-year-old girl who was attending a mixed school said, "The only thing we don't like is that we have had to cut down on social activities like school dances. The Negro children just stay off by themselves."

A 13-year-old girl remarked, "All this year I've only seen one white girl talk to a Negro girl."

In contrast, when I visited rural Prince Edward County, in southern Virginia, I found myself back in an atmosphere of near-wartime conformity. All the public schools in the county stood empty while the white children attended private schools. Virtually everyone seemed determined to keep things that way.

Asked how the private schools were working out, most persons used almost identical phrases in replying, "Better. We've had to cut all the frills, everything but the essentials. No time is being wasted."

One teacher, though, confessed, "There are lots of things about the private schools we don't like. But we keep quiet. This is a struggle of the black man against the white man. I must stick with my own people."

When the school question was put to one florist he said, "Shhh," and pointed to the back of the store where a Negro girl was working. He told his wife to send the Negro girl on an errand. Then he explained, "We can't allow the schools to be mixed. Negro children outnumber us sixty to forty. They'd control the school."

A doctor's wife protested, "We have only one white high school. If you open it, all the Negroes would come in. With us, token integration isn't possible."

In Little Rock, though, I found this same realization as in Norfolk, that "closing the schools hurt the children" and "we couldn't maintain a private school system forever."

One woman, who rang doorbells to get signatures for a petition to reopen the schools, was a divorcee who lost custody of her son when she couldn't give him schooling.

Another man said, "We sent our boy to his grandparents in another state but my wife missed him so much she was crying all the time."

Another father signed a petition to reopen the schools when he discovered that his daughter lacked the credits she needed to get into college.

Other parents said, "It was silly to pay taxes for public schools and then pay for private schools."

I searched out several persons whom I had interviewed in 1958 to see whether their feelings had changed. One factory worker had declared, "I'd rather see Central High School burned to ashes than have it infested with niggers."

But now he felt that, "It makes no difference whether the schools are mixed or integrated as long as they're quiet." Then he added, "It's not what you think. It's what you accept."

An elderly man whom I interviewed in 1958 had sworn, "We will never let any niggers into our schools."

He had branded the Supreme Court as "a bunch of Communists," cursed that "bucktoothed Mrs. Roosevelt," and had talked of bringing economic pressures on the Negroes "to grind them down so they'll come hat in hand and beg for a job." But in 1960 there was little fight left in him. "It's better this way than having the schools closed. He foresaw no more trouble in Little Rock but remarked, "Wait until they start in Mississippi and South Carolina—that will be something to watch."

Moving to Atlanta I found the atmosphere tense, as people waited for the storm to break. The Supreme Court had ordered compliance but the state legislature still held to the position that schools would be closed rather than be desegregated.

Some Atlanta residents gloomily predicted that "the schools will be shut for a year." One Georgia Tech engineer had arranged to send his four children to relatives in other states, "although I don't like their being away from home."

A salesman had taken a second job as a photographer "so I'll be able to put my girl in private school."

One storekeeper's wife complained, "We can't find a private school to take our child. They're all filled up."

In south-side Atlanta a 45-year-old utilities worker apologized. "I'm sorry I can't give you anything but stupid answers but I don't know what to do. I'd like to send my boy to a private school without any colored, "but all the savings I have is a life insurance policy. If I use that now we won't have anything left for the boy's college." His 13-year-old son, who was listening, interrupted, "I'd rather go to school with Negroes than to a private school. If I stay away from them, they won't bother me."

By far the strongest opposition to accepting even token integration came in a south-side precinct, known locally as "a Ku Klux Klan hangout." Some of the families interviewed had drifted into Atlanta from rural Georgia in recent years. A pensioner offered, "I'd give $10 out my pension to help poor people keep their children in private schools."

One housewife vowed, "I'll scrub floors to send my girl to private school."

Another said, "We'll take our kids out of school and teach 'em ourselves as well as we can."

Still others were preparing their children for integration but with much trepidation. A 30-year-old hardware clerk talked of how he was teaching his two sons judo and wrestling. "I want to make sure," he explained, "that when the schools are mixed, the Negroes won't bother my kids more than once. Next Christmas they're going to get boxing gloves."

Still, in all of Atlanta my interviews showed that two of every three parents favored token integration over closed schools. This was in 1960. The following year the schools were integrated without any trouble.

This shift in the terms of racial debate had another important pyschological effect. It enabled moderate opinion in the South to emerge into the open once more. Southerners who had felt unable to speak out for integration could argue vehemently against closing the schools.

And so that was where the South stood in the spring of 1960. Six years of bitter racial warring had finally split the resistance of the South. The less racially sensitive states—Virginia, North Carolina, Tennessee, Florida and Texas—and the larger cities generally were prepared to accept some integration in preference to the disorganization of closed schools.

But the fiercest battles still lay ahead. Whoever succeeded Eisenhower in the White House would have to carry the desegregation struggle into the more rural areas and into the Deep South, where defiance of the Court boiled most intensely.

"Those Freedom Agitators"

In 1935 while the Southern senators were filibustering against a proposed antilynching law, Eleanor Roosevelt brought Walter White to see her husband.

Roosevelt explained to White that "If I come out for the antilynching bill now," the Southerners "will block every bill I ask Congress to pass to keep America from collapsing. I just can't take that risk."

In the spring of 1961 President Kennedy was repeating much the same argument to justify his reluctance to support additional civil rights legislation at that time. Privately he told Negro leaders that such legislation would have to wait until more important bills for which he needed Southern support had cleared.

But if the controlling position held by the South in Congress had not changed in twenty-five years, the temper of the Negroes had.

In a number of cities schools in nonviolence were being conducted. The label "nonviolence" was in many ways an ironic play on words. That the Negroes expected to be treated violently was clear from the training given them: to clasp your hands behind your back if struck; to bring your knees up "toward your chin" if pushed to the ground; "Don't tense up if you're going to be hit," since relaxation eases the blow.

Getting bloodied and beaten, in fact, could be considered an essential part of the strategy of nonviolence. The aim of this strategy, as explained by Negro leaders like Martin Luther King, Jr., is to demonstrate that segregation can no longer be enforced in the South except by constant police repression. An immediate objective is to force negotiation that will bring some change in racial practices. Always in the thinking of the demonstrators is the desire to embarrass our national leaders, to assail the national conscience—and, if possible, to bring on federal intervention, to force the hand of the man in the White House, so that the slow pace of action on civil rights would be stepped up.

The first testing of the Kennedy Administration came in the spring of 1961, when the Freedom Riders started southward, carefully giving Attorney General Robert Kennedy advance notification, in an effort to desegregate bus and travel facilities.

At that time I was already in the South on an interviewing survey. As the headlines of violence at Alabama bus stations built up and President Kennedy was forced to call out the marshals, I probed for the reaction. Would the Freedom Riders widen the split in the South that I had found the year before? Or would the demonstrations boomerang and resolidify the South? What would be the political consequences?

Thanks to a bit of Republican foresight, I found, President Kennedy was not being hurt politically. After Little Rock, Attorney General William Rogers had begun to train a sizable force of U.S. marshals so that they could be used in the South in place of troops. These were the 600 marshals Kennedy sent into Alabama. Many Southerners were pleased by the contrast between the use of these marshals and Eisenhower's calling up troops.

An insurance supervisor in Birmingham opened his wallet and took out a clipping showing paratroopers with drawn bayonets at Little Rock.

"I've been saving that clipping, it got me so mad," he explained. "That turned me against Eisenhower. Kennedy had to act. Our governor couldn't keep violence down. Using marshals was better than calling out troops."

In Greensboro, Nashville, Dallas and Houston three of every four persons interviewed thought the use of marshals was "necessary." In Birmingham and Jackson almost half the persons interviewed felt that "Kennedy had to do something about that mob."

Relatively few persons thought "he should have let the states handle it." On one quiet street in Jackson, Miss., I stopped to talk with a widow who was raking her lawn. Her body shook with anger as she denounced "those Freedom agitators from the North. Why don't they leave us alone?"

Asked how she felt about President Kennedy, she snapped back, "I voted unpledged last time. I'd vote that way twice now."

Beyond some strengthening of third party sentiment, Kennedy was losing relatively few of the voters who had supported him in 1960 and these losses were being offset by shifts of persons who had voted for Nixon. The American voter has always made excuses for Presidents he likes and it was "Brother Bobby" in the Attorney General's office who was blamed for the racial trouble rather than President Jack.

A housewife in Jackson, when asked what was the biggest problem in the country, replied, "Kennedy has too many brothers."

As a result of the Freedom Rider demonstrations the Interstate Commerce Commission ordered "white" and "colored" signs removed from bus and train terminals. But in the Deep South generally, as far as I could determine, the Freedom Riders stiffened the resistance to desegregation. The riders were often referred to as "Red riders" or "friction riders," as "Northern agitators" and "excitement seekers." One Birmingham worker muttered, "The bad thing about the violence was that it didn't scare those coons back north."

In both Jackson and Birmingham the mood of the public seemed much like that of a city under siege. To frustrate the riders, the Jackson police had hit upon a new stratagem, of clapping them into jail before any violence could occur. Everyone I talked with in Jackson knew exactly how many Freedom Riders had been arrested. One local newspaper was running box-score totals of the number of Freedom Rider arrivals, how many had been jailed, how many were out on bail, how many were conducting hunger strikes.

There was a general awareness that the city's strategy was "to keep down violence." In fact, it appeared to have become almost a point of community honor to hold one's anger in check. A restaurant owner remarked, "I'm afraid some hothead is going to kill off one of those niggers. Then Washington will really let us have it."

Three of every four persons interviewed in the two cities said they would close the public schools rather than admit any Negro children.

Most of these persons conceded that "it's coming" or "you can't fight the Federal government and win." But usually such comments would be followed by a vow that "we'll never accept it voluntarily" or "they'll have to force it on us."

Their defiance was not nourished by any serious hope of winning out in the struggle. To the contrary, they seemed resigned to losing out. Still they were determined to delay desegregation until forced to take action and then to act only under compulsion. Declared one Birmingham steel-worker, "Let's close the schools and force the federal government to reopen them."

The old axiom that "you can lead a horse to water but can't make him drink it" seemed to have been given a cock-eyed twist in their thinking. Only by "making them drink it" could many Southerners be got to swallow desegregation.

This sense of embattled solidarity lifted when one moved out of the Deep South into North Carolina, Virginia, Texas and Tennessee.

I had set out on this survey trip to determine whether there was any possible basis of arriving at racial peace. No quick, dramatic reconciliation was possible, of course, but perhaps the two races, despite all their conflicts and clashings, were moving down a road which some years ahead might bring them in sight of a settlement of the issue.

I asked Southerners of every description first:

Do you think this racial struggle must go on indefinitely, with more and more bitterness on each side, or is there some way of settling the whole business?

Then I went on with questions about specific racial practices, to determine on which points white Southeners would yield most readily, on which they would resist most bitterly?

Was it possible to devise an orderly program of gradual desegregation which most white Southerners would be willing to see put into effect during the next five years?

The responses were encouraging, though nothing to cheer about.

There was a general readiness to concede the Negro political and economic rights, but opposition mounted quickly on anything that touched social life.

Table VI shows how the white Southerners interviewed scaled their readiness to see segregation barriers lifted.

TABLE VI. *Attitudes of White Southerners Toward Changes in Racial Customs*

That Negroes should:	% Approve
Vote	95
Work with whites	80
*Go to public schools**	70
Attend same colleges	62
Sit anywhere on local buses	51
Attend same churches	40
Eat in same restaurants	39
Use same swimming pools	9

* On public schools the question asked was, which would you rather have: a few Negroes admitted or public schools shut down?

Nine of every ten white Southerners interviewed opposed Negroes and whites using the same swimming pools. But about as heavy a majority thought that Negroes should be allowed to vote.

Only moderate opposition was voiced to white men working side by side with Negroes, drawing the same pay.

This interviewing was concentrated in Southern cities

and the proportions favoring these changes would be much lower in the rural South. Still the scaling is revealing in that it shows how the same Southerners rate these different practices.

One striking finding was how consistently this scaling was held to in city after city. In Jackson and Birmingham the proportions willing to agree to any program of gradual desegregation were quite small. Still the persons interviewed rated these practices in about the same order.

Even ardent segregationists who replied "no" to every other proposal, and who said, "We have to stand up to the Negro," conceded that Negroes should be able to vote if they could read and write.

At the other end of the spectrum, even liberal-minded Southerners drew the line at desegregating swimming pools. In Richmond, Va., a high school teacher said, "It's time we got something worked out. We have to move faster. The world won't wait." She thought all schools should be mixed. But when asked about swimming pools she replied, "That sets my teeth on edge. I don't think I could get used to that."

Younger Southerners were more ready for change than their elders, Baptists more strongly opposed to easing racial discriminations than Methodists. Only one in five Baptists approved attending the same church as Negroes, while a majority of Methodists did.

A few strong segregationists conceded, "Churches are God's houses, not ours. I'd rather they not come and wouldn't want them to but I'd let them in."

But others argued that "God meant us to be different"

or "It would be good brotherhood but it sure would curdle my churchgoing spirit."

On the question of working together with Negroes blue-collar workers divided almost evenly, while white-collar and professional persons favored it 3 to 1. The strongest objections to working with Negroes seemed to arise from the fear that they might attain positions of authority over whites.

"I don't care but my husband wouldn't like it, I know," said one Atlanta woman. "Imagine having one boss you around."

A Richmond, Va., factory worker said, "I wouldn't want a Negro for a superior at work. I wouldn't want it that way."

Some Southerners thought, "It's all right for Negroes and whites to work together on outside jobs but not in offices with white girls around."

Many objected to eating in the same restaurants because "this is where I take my family." A barber's wife in Greensboro felt, "At these bus terminals Negroes and whites should use the same waiting rooms and eating places but rest rooms should be kept separate. They're too personal."

On the whole, a review of the notes of my 1961 interviewing showed clearly that at least in the moderate South there had been a further relaxation of racial antagonisms as compared to the year before. In North Carolina, Texas, Tennessee and Virginia nearly a fourth of the persons interviewed thought desegregation needed to be pushed faster.

Another half said, "We have to accept some integration" but "Let's give in as little as possible."

The remaining fourth wanted to "do nothing," "just leave things as they are."

Where desegregation had been started, most Southerners were prepared to do more. Many thought that "with Africa the shape it's in we'd better make peace with our own colored people" or "racial trouble gives us a black eye abroad."

Also, for the first time since the Supreme Court's desegregation decision, I found a sizeable number of Southerners saying, "We're sick and tired of all this racial fighting" or "It's time we get our racial troubles worked out."

Politically as well, President Kennedy had come through this first test with strength to spare.

But if gradualism seemed to be winning out in much of the South, the Deep South had not yet been cracked and time was running out.

Turn Against Kennedy

Often on my trips through the South I have thought that textbooks on public opinion need to be rewritten. These texts deal at length with the importance of debate and persuasion, of the relative impact of different media and of the chain of communication through which opinions circulate in a community. Yet throughout the racial war in the South little real debate has taken place. Nor has there been any breakdown in communication.

The main influences molding public feeling have been the structure of Southern society and actual events; perhaps the main forms of communication have been intimidation and violence.

The "massive resistance" of the South was not broken by persuasion but by leaving people no choice between closing the schools or accepting some Negro children. Only when violence forced federal intervention were the Negroes able to gain their rights.

The critical impact of violence and the use of troops in this conflict was impressed on me anew when I returned to the South in the fall of 1963.

Between 1961 and 1963 President Kennedy had had to call out federal troops twice — to ensure the admittance of Negro college students to both "Ole Miss" in Oxford and the University of Alabama at Tuscaloosa.

These two actions almost completely transformed sentiment toward the President. While Brother Bobby was still the main target for Southern abuse, as in 1961, bitter angers were now directed at the President himself.

"Any S.O.B. who would use troops against his own race," cursed one Texan, "isn't fit to be President."

In Birmingham I sampled a workers' precinct which Kennedy had carried in 1960 with a full majority. In a day's interviewing I found only one voter, a 28-year-old Catholic housewife, who was still sticking with Kennedy.

"My neighbors are at me all the time," she said. "It's terrible the things they say about the President. But I think he's right. When I was a child I remember how I used to thank God I was born white."

Everyone else interviewed in this precinct talked of voting either Republican in 1964 or for an independent slate headed by Governer George Wallace of Alabama.

The wife of a plant foreman cursed "that lowdown brother of his" and said "if Kennedy is re-elected it will be the end of America."

When I asked her how she would vote if Governor George Wallace ran as an independent her eyes lit up with zeal.

"He's a wonderful man!" she exclaimed. "He stood up there before that school and told Mr. Kennedy just how I felt."

As I listened to her describe "what a whaling Wallace would give Kennedy" I realized that the performance put on by Governor Wallace before the TV cameras had not been as meaningless as it might have seemed.

To *Time* magazine the Governor, with the lectern in front of him and microphone draped from his neck, seemed to be acting out a "charade" in "an empty gesture of defiance." But other viewers, like this woman in Birmingham, must have projected themselves into his shoes and felt that they were standing in the university doorway telling the President off.

In Jackson a truck driver's wife argued that Governor Wallace actually had a chance to be elected President on a third party ticket. "He's already got Illinois," she said. "I read that in the paper." The story she referred to turned out to be a dispatch from Chicago that petitions were being circulated to put Wallace's name on the Illinois ballot.

Outside of Alabama and Mississippi I found little third party support. Through the rest of the South the struggle was primarily a clash of racial feelings against economic interests. In Fort Worth a 27-year-old mechanic, when asked what is the difference between the two parties, replied, "The Democrats are for high wages and the Republicans are dead against them. Everyone knows that." Still he talked of voting for Senator Barry Goldwater because "a change like this racial thing shouldn't be forced on people."

In Raleigh, N.C., a 41-year-old Greyhound bus driver denounced Kennedy as "a dictator," going on to say, "How can the government have the right to tell a man who he's got to serve? Soon they'll be saying you have to have one out of every ten friends a colored friend." Asked whom he wanted to see elected President, he replied, "I'm a union man and the Democrats are the workingman's party. My union says, much as they dislike to, they'll have to endorse Kennedy if he runs."

Each state seemed to occupy a different rung on this racial versus economic scale. In Alabama and Mississippi anti-Negro feelings blotted out all other issues. But in Texas pocketbook considerations seemed stronger than racial angers. In four Texas cities—Waco, Fort Worth, Dallas and Houston—I found no break in Kennedy's strength. About as many Nixon voters were shifting to Kennedy as Kennedy was losing.

Older people often brought up the memory of the depression as their reason for sticking with Kennedy. A hotel bell captain explained, "I'm against any civil rights law. But in my line it's better to have more money in circulation. Republicans spend tight."

A Houston mechanic protested, "Kennedy flipped his lid for me on integration. But Goldwater is big money. When they balance the budget it hurts the little people."

Strangely enough, despite the political bitterness so evident in the South, I found more openly expressed support for Negro rights than in any previous Southern trip since 1954.

A salesman in a clothing store in Richmond declared, "Kennedy's doing something that has to be done. People should stop raising such an uproar and face up to the fact that Negroes aren't satisfied being maids and porters any more. It's time we did something to help them rather than raise such a stink every time."

A Greensboro housewife confessed, "If I were a Negro I'd do exactly what they are doing. I know I wouldn't like it if I could buy anything from a department store but couldn't get a bite to eat there."

All those who were speaking out for Negro rights were strong supporters of President Kennedy. Many were clearly rallying in defense of the Democratic party. In Columbia, S.C., a textile machinist, who was also the precinct captain, declared:

"Kennedy is doing the *right* thing. My family has been in Columbia for two hundred years. What they've been doing to the nigger is wrong. They've been holding him down like the bosses did to labor until Roosevelt came in. All the nigger wants is a chance to get some dignity. He can't help it if he was born black."

A retired carpenter began the interview by praising medical care for the aged, saying, "Kennedy's thinking of the poor, the old, the retarded. Not many people in his position even give a second thought to poor people. Franklin Roosevelt was another. He did more for the poor people in this country than any man this country ever had."

Asked how he felt about the racial question, this carpenter replied, "Kennedy is doing what the founders of this country intended him to do. I've read the Constitution a few times. They didn't mean for people to go to the back door because they were colored."

In Fort Worth the wife of a city worker recalled, "My grandfather was a nigger hater but I feel that Negroes were brought here. They fight for this country. They should have their rights."

We will never know now what might have happened. Still it was my feeling that, if President Kennedy had stumped the South in 1964 in a calm, straightforward defense of civil rights, the campaign might have had a historic impact. Certainly he would have precipitated a really intensive racial debate throughout the South, perhaps the first such debate on the treatment of the Negro that the South has experienced.

A Psychological War

Looking back over those embattled years, what conclusions can we come to about the nature of Southern resistance to desegregation?

Most impressive, to me at least, is how prodigious has been the psychological turmoil over so small a degree of actual change. After Birmingham the pace of desegregation was stepped up, and 1963 was the first year since the Court's decision that substantial advances were registered. Before that, remarkably little integration had taken place, considering the storms of political fury and personal violence that have been kicked up.

Still, through these years most white Southerners talked as if they were experiencing near-revolutionary changes. Often they protested, "I don't see how we can do any more any faster" when virtually nothing was being done.

Southerners, of course, tend to make a big thing out of even the most trivial racial adjustment. In Barnesville, Georgia, a retired schoolteacher remarked, "I've come a long way from my daddy. He wouldn't let mail be delivered to the house because he didn't want a colored man giving letters to his wife. As for me, I'd let a colored person come to my back door but not to my front door."

Others, like an aged pensioner in Tyler, Texas, feel integration is coming. "But I just don't want to live to see it."

Still others think of themselves, as the schoolteacher in Prince Edward County remarked, as being engaged in a war between the white man and the black man.

The whole racial struggle in the South, in short, has remained primarily psychological. The racial conflict spreading through the North is being generated in the main by upsetting social changes, by the dislocations produced by rising Negro numbers and population shifts. But Southern resistance to desegregation has been provoked mainly by the anticipation of what may come rather than by changes that have actually taken place. The battlefront remains in the minds of the people.

In those Southern communities where desegregation has

taken place resistance has been lessened and not intensified. The fears that were conjured up in advance have not been realized.

Perhaps there is hope in this. If the psychological swords could be beaten into plowshares, quite quick advances might follow. But probably that is why the psychological war continues to be fought so furiously, because the cause of segregation can be held together only by warlike tensions and community conformity, by tight political controls — and an external "enemy."

Delay in implementing the Supreme Court's decision is aggravating rather than easing the difficulties in gaining acceptance. Before open hostilities broke out in 1955 many persons thought there would be proportionately less commotion if small numbers of Negro children were being admitted to the schools — a mere nine at Little Rock, twelve at Clinton, Tenn., eight at Sturgis, only one at Ole Miss.

But political distance is measured not by how far apart two peoples may be but by how conflicting are the directions in which they are pulling. The segregationists were not fighting the number of children involved. They were fighting the idea itself.

The politics of this whole struggle in the South centered around the drive to keep Negroes and whites separate as long as possible.

In making that fight the segregationists forced the adoption of a national racial policy to which they have had to bow; but they also intensified the pressures upon the North to find a way by which Negroes and whites could live together.

Will the battle that was won in the South be lost in the North?

7

The Crisis Moves North

Dead-End Politics

About half a dozen Negro families lived in the Washington suburb of Brookland where Robert Weaver was born. Although a public school stood around the corner, he and his brother had to ride 45 miles each day to attend a segregated school in northwest Washington.

One day Robert returned home to find his grandmother much agitated and on the verge of tears. When he pressed her what the trouble was, she moaned, "There are Negroes moving in on our block!"

Weaver has often related this story to show that Negroes share the identical cravings for snobbish respectability as do white people. They have the same fears as have whites that the streets on which they live will deteriorate, and they are spurred by the same drive to climb into "nicer" neighborhoods.

The failure to satisfy the Negro's urge for better residential surroundings is the crux of the racial crisis in the North. Particularly since the end of World War II the swelling numbers of Northern Negroes have become congested into the larger cities, while white families have been migrating to the suburbs. Between 1950 and 1960 alone the twelve largest cities in the nation lost more than 2 million white residents while they gained nearly 2 million Negro residents. Where in 1950 only one of these cities was as much as 20 percent Negro, by 1960 Negroes made up at least a fifth of the population in seven of these cities, being more than a majority in one, Washington, D.C.

As a result a quite new dimension has been imparted to the racial crisis in the North. In the past Negro leaders have thought their first need was to gain sufficient voting power to make their voices listened to. But Negroes now have that power—as much as a fifth or a fourth of the vote in some cities. Their new dilemma—and it is likely to sharpen in the future—is that this new political power is being exercised in a governmental unit, the suburb-constricted city, which is totally inadequate to meet the Negro's many problems.

The exercise of political power in an ineffective governmental unit—like being the captain of a lifeboat adrift at sea—is bound to prove an agonizing experience for both Negroes and whites. It will place in jeopardy the whole tremendous social and economic investment represented by our major cities.

It is likely to have still further national and even global repercussions as it introduces a new instability into the so-called "big city" vote on which the dominance of the Democratic party has rested. Since 1940 every presidential election has hinged on the majorities won by the Democrats in the main urban centers which dominate the electoral votes of the larger states. Eisenhower's victories were made possible by the fact that he was the first Republican presidential candidate since Franklin Roosevelt who cracked the big cities. In 1964 this big city vote held against Goldwater, but in future elections the solidarity of that vote will be questioned repeatedly by racial stresses and tensions.

The struggle over de facto school segregation provides one revealing illustration of the new dead-end type of politics that is coming to plague Negro-white relations in our major cities. In some of these cities Negro school enrollment has soared to a level where de facto segregation is unavoidable; in other cities that point will soon be reached. Negroes make up nearly 50 percent of the public school enrollment in Detroit, Cleveland and Chicago, 52 percent in Philadelphia, 54 percent in Baltimore, 57 percent in St. Louis.

In New York City the Negro share of the public school population jumped 53 percent in a mere six years, between 1957 and 1963; that of Puerto Ricans rose 37 percent, while white enrollment dropped 8 percent. By 1964 only 30 percent of Manhattan's enrollment was white. No matter where these children attended class, most of Manhattan's schools would be predominantly Negro or Puerto Rican.

In Washington, D.C., where Negroes account for 85 percent of the public school population, hopes of effective integration have had to be abandoned. But in other cities Negro militants have staged demonstrations and boycotts to press more drastic integration proposals, including the busing of white children into Negro schools and the abandonment of the concept of the neighborhood school.

The flareback among white parents has been bitter, even among persons who have always considered themselves advocates of civil rights.

In the Canarsie section of Brooklyn, the 34-year-old wife of a salesman declared, "Segregationists are sick people." But when she was asked about proposals to transfer white children into predominantly Negro schools, she retorted, "I'm against shifting children around like pawns. It's not a question of integration. I don't want my child sent to school in a slum with drunks all around. I don't give a damn whether these drunks are pink or yellow, black or white."

Another mother protested, "My husband and I worked and slaved for years so we could get out of a bad neighborhood. We did it so our children could grow up in a nicer way. Now they want to send our kids back to the filth and squalor we sweated so hard to get out of."

In New Milford, N.J., a 41-year-old salesman argued strongly for opening public accommodations to Negroes in the South. He also wanted the pace of school integration stepped up in the South and said he would not object to Negroes moving in on the same block where he lived. "Separation makes for prejudices because people can't get to know one another," he explained. "Southerners can hate

Negroes but should still give them their rights. We need to show a better face to the rest of the world which is dark."

Still, he went on, "I can't see carrying school kids to another part of town just to prove integration is a good thing. If that's done because a school is overcrowded, it's okay, but not just to have integration. It's not a natural way of doing it. The way to do it is to integrate the neighborhoods."

In several neighborhoods which I visited Negroes were being bused in from overcrowded schools to predominantly white schools which had empty classrooms. Some white parents approved the transfers because "it's good for white children to set an example to Negroes" or "if that's the way of bringing Negroes out of misery it's all right with me."

But more generally the white parents opposed the practice. I found myself probing for the motivations behind their arguments, even as I had done so often in the South.

Two main fears seemed involved.

One was that the school transfers "will pull our children down to the Negro level" rather than raise the quality of Negro schooling. Some parents were worried that the schools might become intellectually unbalanced. Others thought it "okay as long as there is no preponderance of Negroes."

"They're such behavior problems," explained one mother. "Teachers have to spend all the time disciplining them, no time teaching. Around a third Negro is all right. Half and half could be a problem."

A New Jersey high school teacher pointed out, "We have seven Negro families on our block. Their children go to our school. This is gradual, natural integration. We should not bring more Negroes in by bus."

But with many other parents the real objection to busing Negro children into predominantly white schools was, as a Cleveland machinist put it, "I want to keep Negroes from moving into this neighborhood."

In their minds the issue was less the quality of schooling than the desire to hold the prevailing pattern of residential segregation.

Often in protesting the school busing proposals, people would voice sympathy for the racial viewpoint of the South. An insurance salesman in Chicago urged, "Let the South work out its own speed on schools."

A tool grinder in Cincinnati felt, "You have to take it easy with those people." Others thought, "The Negro is pushing too far" or "Integration is going too fast down there."

Virtually no one interviewed knew the actual facts of how little school integration had taken place in the South. Their comments were mainly a reflection of how they felt about the demands that Negroes were pressing locally.

In Chicago, for example, when I asked about the pace of school integration in the South, nearly a third of the persons interviewed replied, "They ought to do it by neighborhood districts" or "Children should go to the schools in their districts no matter what their race is."

In the South, of course, the neighborhood school has never been an issue but it was *the* raging issue in Chicago, where Negro parents were demanding the segregation pattern be broken by having their children bused into predominantly white schools.

From the areas I visited it seemed clear that effective integration could be achieved fairly readily in cities and suburbs where Negroes constitute a small part of the population. In other cities, through rezoning and other administrative devices, it may be possible to keep a higher proportion of white children in some largely-Negro schools. But these "integration" efforts seemed pitifully insignificant when one examined the charts showing the rapid growth of the number of Negro children in proportion to white numbers.

In St. Louis the 1953-1963 decade was marked by a drop of roughly one fifth in white school children and a doubling of the Negroes in the elementary schools. In Philadelphia Negro school enrollment has been rising at the rate of 2 percent a year. By 1980, school board projections indicate, Philadelphia's public school population will be more than two thirds Negro unless there is a dramatic opening up of the suburbs to Negro residences.

These same population trends continue to swell the Negro's voting power. Within another generation, if the suburban-city residential pattern is not changed drastically, Negroes will constitute the largest single voting element in many cities and may even outnumber the white citizenry. Yet, as the Negro numbers rise, it will become increasingly difficult to achieve any real racial desegregation.

Some of my interviewing was done in the fall of 1963 while President Kennedy was still alive, and many normally Democratic voters blamed him for the demands being pressed by Negroes. A Chicago milkman protested, "Kennedy gave them the go-ahead sign." An auto mechanic in Cincinnati said, "He's pushing it too much."

In Detroit an attempt had been made to pass an open-occupancy law which would have required homeowners to sell their property to anyone who offered them the price. A tool and die worker declared, "Kennedy doesn't have to worry about Negroes living next to him. He can outprice any of them. But we can't."

In Philadelphia my interviews on the eve of the 1963 election for mayor showed that a fifth of the voters who had backed Kennedy in 1960 were talking of switching.

One 38-year-old city worker protested, "I was on top of the list for a supervisor's job. Then they made up a new list. They wouldn't let me take the test but gave the job to a Negro who was only three years in the department."

A carpenter said, "They almost moved a colored family in this block. I'm through with Kennedy."

Nearly all of this political anger died down after Kennedy's assassination. Still, the resentments voiced that fall suggest that the Birmingham demonstrations that followed were an important political turning point.

In the past Democratic strategists have assumed that the civil rights issue helped hold together the "big city" vote. This may have been a valid political strategy as long as the civil rights cause appeared mainly a matter of improving the treatment of Negroes in the South.

But the new demands of Northern Negro militants have posed sharp conflicts with what many white voters see as their own rights. Some — no large number — of these white voters shifted to Goldwater in 1964; but many who stayed Democratic did so despite their racial feelings.

In Los Angeles and San Francisco more than half of the persons who voted for Johnson also voted to repeal the Rumford Act for fair housing.

In future elections agitation over civil rights could alienate enough white voters to disrupt the Democratic majorities in the urban areas.

Return of the Machine

During the 1940's it became fashionable to write obituaries of the big city machine. Even Frank Hague, the "I am the law" of Jersey City, had bit the political dust and it was evident that the conditions under which the old-time bosses thrived were gone.

In recent years, however, the big city machine has been staging a comeback, with the Negro as its voting mainstay. Negro immigrants from the South continue to pour into our Northern cities. Many Negroes live in ceaseless entanglement with the law. In addition to their old line of political favors, the political machines now have the modernized wares of welfare state benefits to distribute.

The dependence on the Negro vote for the margin of Democratic victory in some of these cities has leaped prodigiously. When Richardson Dilworth ran for mayor of Philadelphia in 1959, ten predominantly Negro wards supplied only a fifth of his plurality. In 1963 Mayor James H. Tate drew nearly three fourths of his winning plurality in these same wards.

In Chicago the five heaviest Negro wards contributed only a sixth of Mayor Richard Daley's 1959 plurality but more than half of his 1963 plurality.

Eight heavily Negro assembly districts in New York gave Mayor Robert F. Wagner not quite a tenth of his plurality in 1957, nearly four times that in 1961.

Much of the change shown in Table VII reflects the steady alienation of white voters during recent years. In all three

TABLE VII. *Negro Share of Democratic Plurality for Mayor*

	% Democratic	% Plurality in Negro Wards
	New York City	
1957	71	9
1961	52	36
	Chicago	
1959	71	15
1963	55	54
	Philadelphia	
1959	65	21
1963	54	74

cities the normally lopsided Democratic percentages have dropped to 55 percent or less. In Chicago and Philadelphia, Daley and Tate actually won their 1963 victories with the support of a minority of the white voters. Mayor Wagner in 1961 drew less than a majority outside of New York's Negro and Puerto Rican neighborhoods.

Wagner was opposed in the primary by Tammany leaders, and he actually campaigned on the slogan of "Kick out the political bosses." Still a precinct-by-precinct analysis of the primary vote suggests that a new kind of political machine, beholden to the mayor rather than the Tammany bosses, has been taking form in New York City.

One of the best tests of a political boss is his ability to deliver election precincts by overwhelmingly one-sided majorities. In the 1961 primary fight there were hardly 20 election precincts out of 4,000 in all of New York in which the Tammany-allied "bosses" were able to deliver a majority as high as 3 to 1.

By contrast, at least 33 precincts gave Wagner pluralities of 5 and even 10 to 1. Many were public housing projects.

In the November balloting the voters in city-controlled housing projects went 70 percent for Wagner, compared to the 52 percent he drew through the whole city. Predominantly Negro housing projects voted 82 percent for him; the predominantly white projects 63 percent.

In nearly all of our cities the most disturbing political issues boil up out of the tensions and problems generated by the expanding Negro population. In Chicago, where Negroes constitute about a fourth of the population, a special study by the Chicago *Daily News* showed that Negroes account for more than three fourths of the city's arrests for violence, at least 80 percent of all relief recipients and 85 percent of the mothers drawing aid for dependent children. Of these mothers 70 percent have at least one illegitimate child.

In nearly every major city I have checked, the statistics are similar. In Detroit, where Negroes comprise 29 percent

of the population, they account for 79 percent of the welfare
cases, two-thirds of the juvenile offenses and 80 percent of
the mothers receiving aid to dependent children.

The resentments of white families in these cities are
reflected in such common complaints as "It's not safe to
go out into the street after dark" and "Why should we pay
taxes for these people who don't want to work?" But the
strongest anti-Negro sentiments are voiced, I have found, in
homeowning neighborhoods which border on the outer
fringes of Negro residential expansion.

In these neighborhoods each homeowner interviewed
knows exactly on what street the nearest Negro family lives.
Every Negro advance to a new block is regarded as the advance of an enemy army.

Over the past ten years my interviews in neighborhoods
along "the racial frontier" show some small acceptance by
white homeowners of the idea of living alongside of Negro
families. The intensification of racial antagonisms since
Birmingham, I suspect, reflects mainly the fact that old
racial fears are now being pushed to the surface.

A process of racial polarization seems under way, as if
two powerful magnets were passing over these cities, caus-
ing all the iron filings of racial feeling that had been scattered
loosely to cohere suddenly in a white-black confrontation.

This confrontation, in turn, is pushing into the gutter the
old quieter attitude of letting racial relations work themselves out. In its place we are getting conscious conflict and
conscious bargaining.

Among both whites and Negroes, it is well to note, one

finds divided emotions, with attitudes not yet rigidly set. A Cleveland schoolteacher reflected a widespread attitude when she said, "My head says it's a hundred years and things have gone too slow but my heart says they're moving too fast. I don't know what to do."

Actually only a minority of whites can really be classified as being either 100 percent for or 100 percent against the Negro cause. The predominant feeling is one of being torn in conflict. While the post-Selma voting bill was being debated many persons declared, "Voting is one right every American should have," but in the next breath would protest, "I wouldn't want a colored family living near me."

Among Negroes as well considerable differences of feeling exist. In two Philadelphia neighborhoods the Negro parents interviewed were split almost evenly on whether Negro children should be bused into white schools. Some felt, "I ought to be able to send my child to any school in the city." Others argued, "Negro children can get a good education where they are." Several parents were afraid that "teachers in white schools might not like Negro children." A Harlem taxicab driver remarked, "I don't like using kids to fight these battles."

After the Birmingham demonstration I did a survey of Negro feeling in nine Northern communities. About a fourth of those interviewed felt "We ought to hold off on these demonstrations. There might be trouble."

But most Negroes felt that "the white people are scared" and "we have to show them we're through taking it."

Other typical comments ran:

"If it's worthwhile you have to fight for it."

"The black man has his back against the wall. We've got to fight."

These comments were not voiced with revolutionary fervor but more in the tones of workers out on strike who feel, as a New Jersey high school teacher put it, "We're riding high and ought to push for more. We can't give up when we're on top."

A few Negroes whom I interviewed told me, "Be sure to put into your story that there are a lot of Negroes who want to go for violence."

But in none of the Negro neighborhoods sampled did I find real extremist feeling. All but a handful of those interviewed rejected the Muslim doctrines of black supremacy and violence and criticism of Christianity.

A dentist in Canton, Ohio, volunteered, "I know a Black Muslim. I ask him how can a religious man believe one person is better or worse because of color. How can we ask for equality if we say whites are *not* equal?"

A Newark housewife protested, "My religious beliefs won't let me believe that any race is the devil. If a person is a sinner, he's a sinner — black or white."

An unemployed mechanic in New Jersey declared, "I'm an American. I don't want a Negro country. I want to stay in this one."

A twenty-seven-year-old minister in Youngstown felt, "You can't fight hate with hate."

An unemployed electrical worker in Brooklyn thought, "This violence business is silly. We're outnumbered. We couldn't win."

More revealing perhaps was what the Negroes liked about the Black Muslims. Perhaps one in every ten Negroes said something favorable about the Muslims. Nearly always it was a reference to the self-discipline imposed on Muslim members. "They stop Negroes from using dope when doctors can't," or, "They help the Negro by giving him self-respect."

A twenty-three-year-old housewife in Pittsburgh revealed, "The Muslims stopped my two brothers from drinking. But I don't go along with black supremacy. Everyone should be equal. The Negro has too much to lose if separated."

The strength of the Black Muslim appeal, in short, seems to lie in the lift it gives to Negro pride. This quickened pride was, of course, the main attraction of Garvey's movement. Of the many things the white man denies the Negro, it is pride that he prizes most highly.

One other point should be noted about the Negro reaction in the months after Birmingham — at that time the rank and file of Negroes were considerably less militant than their leaders. There has been a tendency to radicalize the Negro masses in the North through a competition of militancy among Negro leaders. The bolder demands of the newer, younger militants have forced even organizations like the NAACP and the National Urban League to become more belligerent.

Some civil rights leaders feel themselves in competition with one another in raising funds; others talk of Negroes joining a "social-change coalition" pledged to reorganize the whole of society; still others urge militancy for its own sake.

These newer militants often direct their taunts of "Uncle Tom" at the older established leadership, or at Negroes who hold government or union posts. In several cities like Chicago and Philadelphia there have been clashes with the Democratic machines. Chicago Negro "boss," Congressman William Dawson, has used his appreciable powers to oppose school boycotts and other agitations. In the course of this struggle Dawson infiltrated and gained control of the Chicago chapter of the NAACP. Some of the hostility directed by Negroes at Mayor Daley reflects resistance to Dawson's dominance.

In Philadelphia the newer militants, like Cecil Moore who has been pressing economic boycotts, have been feuding with the Negroes who stand highest in the Democratic party.

This political restlessness will bring some Negro "bolts" from the Democratic party but for these insurgencies to become a lasting force, racialism would have to become the dominant consideration in the minds of Negro voters, overriding appeals of government benefits, union membership and the patronage of the big city machines.

The really troubling feature of this competition of militancy among Negro leaders is that there is no possible way, even with utmost good will, of delivering *fully* on Negro demands for "freedom now." The agitations of the Negro militants are being spurred less by a desire for specific reforms than by a *general* sense of grievance which inclines them to push and push until they meet resistance. One young Negro remarked, "How do I know you're discriminating against me until I sit down next to you and see what you do?"

There is sore need for greater vigor in tackling each specific problem that afflicts Negroes. Still, whatever is done will hardly dent the mountains of neglect that time has heaped up. Even a decade ago the needed adjustments could have come so much easier.

The Great Separation

Few American beliefs are more strongly held than the thought that economic improvement constitutes a magic ointment which will eliminate or at least relieve any and all social ills.

Yet it is the unbroken prosperity of the postwar years that stirs at the bottom of much of the racial crisis in the North. This prosperity has tightened the pattern of residential segregation and widened the gulf between Negro and white families, even while quickening Negro demands. In the process it has also weakened the ties that bind the voting elements in the New Deal coalition.

The key explanation can be stated simply. As far as race relations are concerned, the level of the economy is of secondary importance. Whatever economic standing a Negro achieves, he is never accepted automatically or unconsciously as white persons are. He faces one additional problem, that of fitting himself into the structure of society. This need of a "structural fit" dogs him regardless of what his earning power or education may be.

The evidence of the postwar years even argues that hard times and adversity may make it easier for the Negro to find this structural fit. It was the depression, with its breadlines and apple vendors, that for the first time in American history enabled white and black workers to find a common sense of economic interest.

In contrast, between 1940 and 1955, the per capita cash income of Negroes more than tripled; white-collar employment among Negroes rose half again as much as it had been; homeownership leaped 137 percent, to where every third Negro family owned its own home. But this economic advance, along with similar gains by white Americans, has helped produce a Great Separation of whites and blacks that will probably take a full generation or more to heal over.

In physical terms this Great Separation can be seen most vividly in the contrast between the relatively few Negroes who have joined white families in suburban home developments and the swollen numbers of Negroes who have remained dammed back in the central cities. And this separation has been psychological and political as well as physical.

For one thing the Northern Negro has remained the only major element in the New Deal coalition subject to continued immigration. The older minorities have been able to move into the middle class, with their immigrant past a closed chapter. Negroes, though, have had to bear the continued burden of fresh emigration from the South.

This influx has made it difficult for Negroes who had bettered their economic status to maintain an identity separate from lower-income Negroes. Pushed together by residential segregation, middle- and lower-class Negroes tend to be lumped as one in the white society's imagery.

The suburban exodus also broke another common link of Negro-white experience—shared memories of discrimination. Being so largely the children and grandchildren of immigrants, most of the Democratic voting elements had suffered discrimination in their youth. They had been denied employment because of the sound of their family names. Having shared the experience of being insulted almost daily as "wops" or "micks" or "kikes" or "hunkies" or "spicks," they had a common stake in wanting to eliminate racial and religious intolerance.

By moving to the suburbs most white families left the "old world" of discrimination. For the middle-aged parents, the old taunts faded into nostalgic memories; while the newer generation growing up in the suburbs would find it difficult even to understand that discrimination was not just a word in the dictionary.

Negroes, though, were left behind in the old prison of prejudice, left in almost solitary confinement.

The prosperity of the war and postwar years also enabled a sizable proportion of the white families to shift from renting apartments to owning homes. Presumably this change improved living habits and perhaps even made better fathers and mothers—though this remains to be documented. But the rise in status from banging on the radiators for steam heat to fighting crab grass did not lower racial prejudice. On the contrary, it seems to have topped the already high walls of segregation with the barbed wire of property consciousness.

In rental areas, my interviews show, people are less likely to panic and flee if Negro families move into the same street. The white families know they can get out easily enough whenever they want to. Homeowners, though, dread that property values may tumble and much of their savings be lost if ownership on a street changes too swiftly from white to Negro.

These fears of the homeowner may well be the strongest single source of white resistance to Negroes in the North today. During my interviewing in the summer and fall of 1963

I questioned people systematically on how they felt about specific rights which Negroes wanted: the right to a job without discrimination, to have restaurants and hotels open to Negroes, to send their children to predominantly white schools, and "to buy a home on the same street where you live."

Ten in every eleven persons interviewed replied "no" to the idea of Negroes being able to buy alongside of them. In contrast, only one in ten opposed the idea of Negroes being able to work at any job for which they were qualified.

In Akron a retired Goodrich worker recalled, "I put my house up for sale last year. A Negro drove by and looked at the sign. The woman across the street told all the neighbors I was going to sell to Negroes. They came and asked me not to. My real estate man said he had a woman who wanted to look at the place who was Negro. He said he'd lose his job if he didn't send her over. She never came but if she had I would have told her it was already taken or something."

In Los Angeles an aircraft worker said, "If a Negro moved into this block I'd like to think I'd stay. But if my neighbors panicked I guess I'd run too."

Other people said, "I wouldn't mind one colored family in the block but I wouldn't want to be a minority in a colored neighborhood" or "One family would be okay but soon another would come in and then another."

A few persons recalled a time when living alongside of Negroes had not troubled them. The wife of a factory supervisor in Cleveland remarked, "It's funny. I was raised with Negroes in the old neighborhood. I played with them and didn't think anything of it. When times were hard you had to live where you could."

Some families told of having moved several times in recent years to get out of neighborhoods that had become colored. A few asked wearily, "How long can you keep running?" Others seemed to have been stiffened in their determination to live separate from Negroes.

Sometimes, in fact, the arguments sounded exactly like those I had heard in the South. In Brook Park, on the outskirts of Cleveland, a truck driver's wife maintained, "Negroes should have rights but we shouldn't be forced to live alongside them. I wouldn't want my daughter marrying one. If the children play together, sure enough one out of ten will marry one."

Resistance to living near Negroes seems to pack the same emotional equivalent for Northerners that school integration does for Southerners.

The fact that this Great Separation between the cities and suburbs has come into being has become a force in itself in keeping the races apart. To many persons the line that divides cities from suburbs is a Berlin-like wall. On the city side of the wall the spectacle is one of spreading slums, ever-blacker Negro concentrations, ever-heavier burdens of social problems. On the suburban side, all the indices of social trouble are lower, the concentrations of slums or Negroes relatively scarce.

Students of government have written dire predictions of urban chaos unless the cities and suburbs can be merged into some kind of consolidated metropolitan authority. With few exceptions, though, such consolidation proposals have been rejected by the voters.

Suburbanites, who have fled the cities to escape delinquency, heavy welfare loads and high taxes, shudder at the thought of taking on the problems of the central cities. On their end, Negroes also have tended to vote against metropolitan mergers for fear that the political power they now wield in the central city would be watered down inside a larger governmental unit.

This intertwining of racial antagonisms with governmental units is a deeply menacing development. At best it aggravates the difficulties of assimilation; at worst, as shown by the history of the South, it can lead to psychological and even social war. Perhaps it is not too late to halt this trend, but in every major metropolitan area we seem to be digging deeper the fortifications for continued racial war, aligning governments answerable to whites against governments answerable in the main to Negroes.

That this has happened in a period of booming prosperity is worth re-emphasizing. The essence of our racial crisis is not economic, as so many Americans like to believe, but structural, reflecting the walls in our minds and in our society that separate whites and blacks.

Nor can it be emphasized too strongly that no force of progress will topple these barriers for us. The walls can be brought down only by our own conscious efforts to readjust the structure of our living and thinking.

Outside the Economic Fortress

This same need for a "structural fit" emerges when one analyzes the Negro's job problems. The rate of unemployed among Negroes is put twice as high as among whites. Much of this is caused by the discrimination that Negroes suffer. But it is also important to note that Negro unemployment reflects the same influences that explain joblessness among whites.

During the spring of 1963 I did a special survey of unemployed workers in 23 cities. One main purpose was to try to discover why the jobless rate in the nation remained so high — then well over 5 percent of the labor force — in the face of record highs in production, employment and consumer spending.

Much of the explanation, I found, was that the bulk of the unemployed were not in the mainstream of the nation's economic life. Mainly they were older workers who had been pushed out of the economy and younger workers who had never been able to get set on any job.

The fact is that we seem to have developed two almost separate economies in this country — one a highly protected, employment-secure fortress and the other an exposed plain that is raked whenever there is economic trouble.

The contrast with the Great Depression is worth emphasizing. In the depression years, as the economy recovered, the available jobs went to the newer, younger workers, while many middle-aged and elderly workers never were rehired.

During recent years, however, the middle-aged, highest-seniority workers have been steadily tightening their control over the available jobs while the brunt of unemployment has been thrust upon the younger, newer workers outside of the seniority fortress.

In nearly every city I found something of a "wasted generation" of young people — white and black — who were pushing thirty and even thirty-five years of age and still had never held a steady job since leaving school.

In my analysis of the Negro workers interviewed I divided them into two groups: those who voiced confidence that they soon would be back at work and those who complained "I keep looking but get nothing."

Each group had an equal proportion of high school graduates. What distinguished the gloomy Negroes was the fact that they generally were younger and had held non-manufacturing jobs like elevator operators, car washers or porters. Two thirds of them had worked less than a year for their last employer.

In St. Louis, for example, two Negro brothers were standing in line at the unemployment compensation center. Both had worked as paint sprayers in a trucking firm for five months. They had been fired for being absent from work for several days. The younger brother had held three previous jobs in three years out of school. The older brother had gone through four jobs in three years. Much the same pattern was evident among the younger white workers. Although much of my interviewing was done in major industrial centers, like Detroit, Akron, Pittsburgh, Cleveland and St. Louis, few of these youths had ever worked for one of the bigger companies. The overwhelming majority had been compelled to forage for jobs among the scrub pines of smaller, shakier employers, at relatively low pay and "with no union to protect you."

In a fifth of the cases at least one firm they worked for had folded. Others had been employed by "family affairs" and "got bumped to make room for the boss's relatives."

In Newark, N.J., one youth remarked, "I'd like to be an electrician but you've got to be the first-born son of a union member to get a union card."

At the Minneapolis unemployment center one 20-year-old remarked, "It may sound funny to you but I often wake up at night from a dream in which I've at last got a union card."

In Chicago a 27-year-old who had bounced among three jobs during one year exclaimed with fervor, "I sure would like to work for a big company! You know where you stand."

After checking through 350 case histories, I felt that too much emphasis has been put on the difficulties of limited education and lack of vocational skills. Not enough attention has been given to the fact that younger workers have been virtually walled out of employment in many trades and the major manufacturing industries by the structure of union benefits and seniority that has been built up in recent years.

The young people who do manage to get past the fortress walls face a rough period at the start. Being the last hired, they are the first to be fired if any slowdown occurs. Often the same men will get fired year after year, while the older workers put in full hours and even overtime without being touched by layoffs.

Still there is little revolt against this system. The overwhelming majority of workers accept seniority as a crude, impersonal form of machine age justice. They reason that if they can sweat it out long enough they will eventually acquire enough seniority to be secure.

Often the younger workers count the number of retirements that must take place for them to become permanent workers.

In Dearborn a 35-year-old truck driver took out his unemployment compensation book and counted up "only ten weeks of work this year." He explained: "Under our Teamster contract my company guarantees every regular driver forty hours of work. But ten per cent of the drivers are called casuals. I'm one. We work when an extra driver is needed, maybe for a day, maybe a week."

Still this driver was pleased with the arrangement. "I get $3.13 an hour when I work," he said. "When enough of the older fellows retire I'll become a regular driver. That will fix me for life." Asked how long that would take, he replied, "At least five years. I'll be forty-one before I can count on steady work. Still, before I got this job, it didn't look like I'd ever get anywhere."

In some industries, like steel and autos, the companies pay supplementary unemployment benefits so that workers draw better than two thirds of their pay even when laid off. Those who are laid off do little hunting for a new job—unless it is for odd jobs that do not show up in taxable payrolls—and simply wait to be recalled.

At West Homestead a steelworker calculated that "since 1958 I've been out half the time." Still, "If I went anywhere else I'd be low man on the totem pole and would be laid off every time there was a slowdown. This way every year brings me closer to the day when I'll have enough seniority to work all the time."

A factory worker in New Haven, Conn., when asked why he didn't look for a job in another line, replied "who would hire me? They know I'd go back to my old company as soon as work picked up."

The really harsh years for younger workers were those between the 1958 recession and the boom that took hold in 1963. Since the seniority system required companies to recall workers who had been laid off, few new workers were brought into most manufacturing industries. What this did to the younger people — white and black — who were entering the labor market can be seen in some statistics I collected from some of the larger auto and steel companies.

Before the 1958 recession 7.1 percent of all steel workers were under 25 years of age; in 1962 only 4.8 percent were. By the end of 1964 though, the proportion of workers under 25 had leaped to 10 percent.

The records of one large auto company shows that 19.2 percent of its workers were under 25 in 1955. By 1961 the proportion had dropped to 8.5 percent. In 1963, the latest year for which figures are available, the under-twenty-fives were 13 percent of the hourly working force.

The creation of nearly three million new manufacturing jobs between 1963 and 1965 opened the fortress gates to many younger workers. But the fortress walls still stand — and the gaps in living between those who are in the protected part of the economy and those who wait outside is perhaps greater than ever.

A strange feast-or-famine paradox confronts the younger job seekers. While some are accepted into industries with high pay and liberal fringe benefits, others, often their friends, find themselves stamped as "human rejects."

In Columbus, Ohio, I spotted a young man proudly polishing a new car. He had quit school in the eleventh grade and gone into the service. After that he bounced about for two years as a part-time cook, stock boy and produce clerk.

Then an opening developed with the railroad for which his father worked. With this new job the life of this dropout changed magically. He was able to get married and buy a house and a brand-new car, all inside of two years.

"I feel funny," he confessed. "If not for my 'in' with the railroad I'd be down in the dump. My best friend can't get regular work. They keep telling him he needs a high-school diploma."

Each year at least three million more youngsters are expected to reach working age. Nearly a fifth of these will be Negroes. The more new jobs that are generated, the easier it will be to place these youngsters in the economy. But the experience of the 1963-65 period suggests that even a booming economic growth will not overcome their difficulties.

The better qualified youngsters will be hired first, while

those still out of work will tend increasingly to drain down into "marginal" workers with marked personal difficulties. In my 1965 unemployment survey nearly a tenth of the jobless workers interviewed fell into this category. Some had physical defects, like a cleft lip or one eye, or had suffered disabilities. A garment-presser in New Haven remarked, "Since my accident my right arm isn't as fast as it was."

A Pittsburgh man had become an alcoholic because "my wife could not have any babies." Still others had a wanderlust which kept them moving from job to job. Said one 45-year-old maintenance man, "I never stick anywhere long. I want to go some place where your mind can't stay in one spot."

Three antipoverty projects I checked — in Los Angeles, Newark, N.J., and New Haven, Conn. — yielded some inspiring tales of success. One 17-year-old New Haven boy, with a police record, had been expelled from school and kicked out of his home. He was put to work in a Nature Center where he developed an interest in flowers. He now is working for a florist full time and seemed to be doing well.

But it was also clear that many of these youngsters could not really be considered problems in employment — they simply hadn't worked themselves up that high.

Some were still sunk in delinquency, social and even mental problems. In one sampling of young people assigned to a Newark project, more than half had dropped out or been expelled. Several proved to be mental cases; nearly a dozen became sick or pregnant; still others persisted in their delinquency even after being assigned to a work project.

Of the youngsters who did stay in the program, more than half were making good progress.

No one knows what part of the total youthful "slum dynamite" in the major cities is "unemployable" in their present condition, in need of psychiatric or social care rather than a job. Certainly the number is sizable.

Another danger is that the barriers to employing young people may be raised not lowered. Employers, seeking an easy form of rejection, tend to impose arbitrary hiring qualifications, such as demands for ever-higher educational qualifications, even when these are not needed to perform the work.

Union resistance to youngsters may also be intensified. Younger people will be eager to work at wage rates far below the prevailing level, not simply to get work but because these younger people don't think they're worth more. Labor unions are likely to respond to this threat by tightening the screws of control over the available jobs and by pushing ever higher the wages and fringe benefits for their members.

This is what has happened in the past. Each new union contract has tended to raise ever higher the walls of the protected part of the economy. Wage and fringe benefits have been pushed to the point where many companies figure it is cheaper to pay overtime than to hire a new man and foot his insurance, hospitalization and other benefits. In several unemployment centers young workers told of being hired for temporary jobs and being "dropped the week before I could qualify for fringe benefits."

If changes are made in retirement or overtime practices or

in the working week, these benefits are likely to be swallowed up by the union members with little easing of the plight of the workers still left outside the fortress.

The whole process of collective bargaining should be re-examined in the light of this clash between the needs of the younger workers and the claims of the workers long on the job. Labor unions naturally are concerned with the welfare of their own members. At present in the bargaining for contracts no one really represents the public interest.

Union demands are often publicized as being framed to create more work, but there is no one sitting in at these bargaining sessions to see that contract terms do not lift higher the fortress walls and narrow rather than widen employment opportunities.

Often as well the unions thwart or weaken retraining efforts. This obstructionism has been most flagrant in California where not a single training course in auto mechanics and auto repairs was being offered as late as the spring of 1965. In the rest of the nation this has been easily the most popular single type of job training for males.

A faster rate of economic growth will not eliminate this need for an all-out assault on these and other discriminations to employment. If anything economic growth is likely to sharpen the problem of discrimination. A two-handed giant, economic growth creates new jobs with one hand even while it renders obsolete old jobs with the other hand.

For those who are pushed out of the economy, the result can be a stubborn, hard-core kind of unemployment. Some are told, "you're too old" when they apply for new work. Even persons as young as thirty-five have told me of being passed over for that reason. Others must forget their old trades and take anything that is offered. Often these are only spare, short-time jobs which bring a man back to the unemployment line year after year.

Rapid technological change can be doubly harsh for the Negro. For always he labors under the special vulnerability that his color makes it difficult to fit himself into a new job situation.

A rapid rate of economic growth can also be expected to encourage the shifting of factories from one part of the country to another.

Ironically, except for California, the heaviest Negro migrations in recent years have been into states which have been losing industry to the South. Between 1950 and 1960 the eight Northern states with the highest Negro numbers — Illinois, Maryland, Michigan, New Jersey, New York, Ohio, Pennsylvania and California — increased their Negro population by 55 percent while the number of manufacturing jobs rose only 16 percent.

The Southern states, which have been losing Negro population, were able to raise the number of their nonagricultural jobs by 32 percent between 1950 and 1960.

To sum up, the job crisis that confronts the Negroes seems compounded by three main influences. There are the harsh handicaps that Negroes bear because of discrimination and, as part of the legacy of past discrimination, less education and fewer skills.

At the same time the unskilled and semiskilled jobs for which Negroes qualify most easily have not been increasing as rapidly as other jobs.

But much of the Negro's problems must also be attributed to the fact that new rigidities have been introduced into our economic structure in the form of strengthened unions and higher worker benefits, also in the disparities that have developed in the ability or inability of different segments of the economy to pass on rising costs to the consumer.

Paradoxically, the essence of these job security provisions is discrimination, discrimination in favor of those who control the job monopoly or the job security machinery.

The fact is that we no longer have a truly free economic society in the United States. Most of us would not want to see these job security arrangements scrapped and the 1920's and 1930's brought back. But that fact in itself undercuts faith in automatic progress, in the belief that a booming prosperity will solve the Negro's employment problem.

No matter how high an economic level is hit, conscious efforts will still have to be made to fit the Negro — and many younger white workers as well — into the economic structure.

Some Negro leaders, like Whitney Young of the National Urban League, have urged that Negroes be given preferential treatment in job hiring as compensation for the past discriminations they have suffered. I do not think it is right for a government to say one man should be preferred to another because of his color or lack of color. Our energies should be directed at leveling the walls of discrimination that now exist and in helping Negroes become more efficient workers.

Negro militants can be expected to continue to push for more wherever they can. Perhaps that is how we should look on the picketings, sit-ins, marches and even Negro riotings

—as a new form of collective bargaining. This bargaining seems aimed at overcoming the weaknesses of Negro representation in the political process, in existing trade unions, in being dealt with by the police, in the economy generally. The disorganization exhibited by Negro militants can be compared to the wildcat strikes that accompanied the first labor organizing drives in the early New Deal years.

But if this parallel is valid it poses a critical question for the future: what long-run forces can be looked to as a means of narrowing the racial cleavage?

With workers and employers the bitter antagonisms of the 1920's and early New Deal years were blurred over gradually and made less intense by economic improvement on the worker's part and other developments such as the steady climb toward middle-class comforts and the expansion of white-collar workers in contrast to factory employment.

But racial bargaining poses a wholly new challenge to the American people. In its first impact it has sharpened the sense of cleavage and separateness among Negroes. Many Negro leaders, in fact, are using the racial crisis to try to organize the Negro community into a hostile bargaining force against the white community. This tactic is even being encouraged by the government. Under the poverty program, Negroes are being organized for "community action" — which means staging rent strikes and picketing city agencies for improved services.

With minority groups, hostility is often a spur to achievement, and strengthening Negro bargaining power could help eliminate prevailing abuses. But there lurks always the special danger of perpetuating the Negro's sense of racialism. Negro pressures and white resistance can readily degenerate into tests of strength which will only widen further the white-black cleavage. Some higher principles are needed to guide the bargaining.

Before turning to what might be done in this regard, let us examine one other matter: the likely impact of the "Negro Revolution" on both the Democrats and the Republicans. Can our political parties prove sufficiently ingenious to transform the raging conflict into a unifying, nationalizing force? And if not, what does lie ahead?

8

The Politics of Race

Mona Lisa Southerner

One intriguing feature of the public's first reaction to Lyndon Johnson becoming President was the revelation of how much of our political thinking is done in symbols, to which we attach our prejudices and interests, our hopes and fears.

To loyal Kennedy supporters the new President's opening speech to Congress was assurance that "he'll hold to the liberal line." But to other voters the significant symbol was Johnson's being "a Southerner," which to them meant "He's bound to be more conservative" than Kennedy had been.

While Negroes were delighted with the President's pledge to fight for Kennedy's civil rights bill, most Southerners dismissed the pledge as "something Johnson had to say" and felt certain "he's bound to go slower" on civil rights.

The fact that he was a Southerner succeeding Kennedy, in short, gave Johnson the political equivalent of that mystifying Mona Lisa half-smile into which everyone could read his own hopes and expectations.

This early voter reaction to Johnson left little doubt that he would be able to bring at least temporary unity to the Democratic party. Throughout the South, which had been rumbling with political fury against the Kennedy brothers, there was an immediate upsurge of enthusiasm. Some Southerners were stirred with pride over having the first lifelong Southerner as President since Abraham Lincoln's assassination put another Johnson (Andrew) into the White House.

"He sounds like one of us!" exclaimed a limousine driver in Greensboro, N.C.

An airport attendant at Raleigh remarked, "When Johnson quotes from the Bible I know he's like the people I was raised with."

Other voters explained their shift to Johnson by saying "I went against Kennedy because he was a Catholic. But I'm still a Democrat."

But probably the key reason for Johnson's popularity in the South in those days was the almost universal expectation that "he won't push as hard" as Kennedy did on civil rights. To Southerners generally, Kennedy, and even more so Brother Bobby, had come to symbolize an extreme pro-Negro position. A factory foreman in Birmingham summed up the feeling of much of the South when he remarked, "That was a rotten way for Kennedy to go, but I'll be frank with you, I think Johnson will be a big improvement. He understands the South."

With this feeling, though, went a readiness to accept more of a civil rights program from Johnson than would have been taken from Kennedy. In the first few weeks after Kennedy's death, seven of every ten Southerners interviewed thought "some law has to be passed."

The feature of the bill which provoked deepest concern was the provision that would open to Negroes hotels, restaurants and other public places. In Richmond, Va., a college janitor who also owned a restaurant voiced a typical protest, "It's taking my rights and giving them to others. If they come into my place my white customers may go somewhere else. They could put me out of business."

"I'd let Johnson have it," said one Louisiana builder, "if I thought he wouldn't enforce it."

This readiness of Southerners to accept moderate civil rights legislation was not as suprising as it might seem. Actually, only a minority of Southerners, mainly in Mississippi and Alabama, have believed that desegregation could be halted completely. Their best hope has long been to slow down the process. "We'll get it no matter who is President," was the commonly voiced feeling. "Maybe Johnson will do as well for us as anyone could."

That Southern resistance could flare up again quite quickly was made clear by the responses given me to the question: "What if Robert Kennedy is named for Vice-President with Johnson?"

More than a third of the pro-Johnson supporters declared, "I'd vote against Johnson if Bobby Kennedy runs with him."

Typifying their angry reaction were remarks like these:

"Running Bobby Kennedy would be hitting the South below the belt."

"I'll never take a chance on a Kennedy becoming President again."

"He's not for the white man."

The passage of the civil rights law in mid-June of 1964 brought an abrupt change in the feeling of many Southerners towards Johnson.

Shortly after Kennedy's assassination, a veterinarian in Greensboro had told me, "I feel secure with Johnson in the White House. He understands us. Those Kennedy brothers were destroying the country."

In July of 1964, though, when this veterinarian was re-interviewed he was strong for Goldwater. He explained, "Johnson was too hasty with that civil rights law. We don't like having things pushed down our throats."

On the next street a steelworker declared, "I'm a Democrat but right now I'd vote for Goldwater. I don't want my kids going to the same swimming pools as coloreds."

The winter before, this same steelworker had praised Johnson, saying, "The Supreme Court will be pushing him, but Johnson will go as slow as he can with civil rights."

This turn against Johnson would probably have not been so sharp but for Goldwater's vote against the civil rights law and his being nominated by the Republicans. The San Francisco nomination sent a new current of militant political revolt through the South. In Fayetteville, N.C., a 49-year old furniture dealer who had never voted for a Republican President, summed up this change when he exclaimed, "At last the South has a choice!"

"No past election excited me," he explained. "Both parties were after the colored vote. Who cared who won? But when

Goldwater told those New Yorkers at the Republican convention that they could leave the Republican party if they didn't
like his civil rights views, I knew that at last we had someone
who will fight for us."

Other Goldwater supporters in the South declared, "We'll
win with Barry and repeal that terrible niggers' rights law" or
"This is the time for the white man to make his stand."

That July I heard more open talk of realigning party loyalties in the South than in any previous election campaign. In
Fort Worth a 56-year old mechanic declared, "The Republican party now stands for all the things the Democrats used
to represent."

A retired carpenter in Richmond protested, "I've always
voted Democratic before, but the Democrats just moved in on
me with a wheelbarrow and took my party away."

Many other Southerners, when asked about their party
feeling, replied, "I vote for the man" or "put me down as a
conservative." An oil well driller in Houston said, " I want to
go back to the kind of government which doesn't tell people
how they have to live."

In those first weeks after the GOP convention, many
Southerners also thought that Goldwater would sweep the
South and even win in the whole nation. The vote drawn by
Governor Wallace in Democratic primaries in Indiana, Mary-
land and Wisconsin had been headlined as evidence of a
sizable white backlash in the Northern cities. The common
Southern expectation — or hope — was that this "backlash"
could be allied with Southern racial resentments.

In the early summer such a merger seemed at least possible.
My first interviews in six Northern states showed that racial
angers and tensions were cutting in heavily on the Johnson

vote. Of those who had voted for Kennedy, one in seven talked of shifting to Goldwater.

Even families who had stayed Democratic through the two Eisenhower landslides talked of breaking. In Jackson Heights, N.Y., a paint sprayer's wife declared, "I've voted Democratic all my life, but I'm sick of these Negroes telling the government what to do."

Another lifelong Democrat said he would shift to Goldwater because "a Negro sat down next to my wife in the subway and blew smoke into her face."

A chef in Jersey City protested, "Every time my car stops next to a Negro's, I'm afraid bricks will be thrown at me. This has to end. I want peace."

In southeast Chicago, the precinct I selected at random turned out to be one which was just beginning to experience the agonies of block-busting.

"Some Negroes killed a white woman up the block," explained one resident. "Since then the real estate agents keep calling us asking don't we want to sell before the block turns black."

Half the Democratic voters on these streets talked of voting for Goldwater. A 63-year old factory worker explained, "I'm troubled that Goldwater is against labor and Medicare. But the other day a Negro offered only $11,000 for a house on this block. If I sold at that price I'd lose all my savings."

Down the street a retired man was working on the flower beds in his back yard. "Right now I'm leaning to Goldwater," he said. But I hope the Negroes moving in will be good neighbors. I want to stay here."

As I turned to leave, he pointed to his gladioli and remarked wearily, "Every fall I dig up the bulbs and replant them in the spring. I've been doing that for 20 years. But this year I guess I'll let the bulbs stay in the ground."

But this white backlash didn't hold up through the campaign. Somehow the word went out through the Negro community that rioting had to be stopped unless the Negroes wanted Goldwater in the White House and the riotings did stop.

In Canton, Ohio, a 25-year old mechanic, who had praised Goldwater's vote against the civil rights law in July, decided to stick with the Democrats because "there are no more riots. The coloreds know now they can't move so fast."

Similarly a pensioner's wife in Gary, Ind. had also decided not to vote for Goldwater after all, because "we don't like niggers but Kluxers are worse."

Many other voters had been worried that a Goldwater victory might aggravate rather than ease the racial turmoil in the country. In Rochester, which had been torn by rioting, I sampled a precinct that bordered on a Negro area. A 31-year-old electrician who was also the Republican precinct captain, recalled that while the rioting was going on "I sat on my door-step with a baseball bat in case any Negroes came barging down our street."

Still, he talked of resigning as precinct captain rather than campaign for Goldwater.

"We have to accept the colored people," he explained. "If Goldwater won we'd have racial war in this country and war abroad."

A car repairman in Pittsburgh, a postal worker in Syracuse, a real estate salesman in Canton, a polisher in Buffalo, an apartment house owner in Chicago — all voiced the same fear: "Goldwater is so much against Negroes, we could have terrible trouble if he wins."

With other voters, as the campaign progressed, racial angers became less urgent than other fears which Goldwater stirred.

In the Canarsie section of Brooklyn, N.Y., the owner of a shoe repair shop had joined in keeping his child out of school to protest against white children being bused into predominantly Negro schools. Still he and his wife were voting for Johnson.

She explained, "I think Goldwater is crazy. With civil rights only half the world is blowing up. With Goldwater it would be the whole world."

A boilermaker in Philadelphia recalled how his car had been damaged in the Negro rioting there and swore, "Johnson is too much for the niggers!"

"But we have no choice," he added. "Goldwater is such a maniac."

In Canton, an auto salesman's wife recalled, "We wanted to vote for Goldwater because of his courage in going against the civil rights law. But now we're afraid of him. He seems unstable."

Outside the South a full third of the persons who said they would vote for Lyndon Johnson also thought, "Negroes are pushing too hard" and "that civil rights law should not have been passed."

But the *coalition* nature of American political parties brings together voters who may disagree violently over one issue and still be held together by other cementing appeals.

THE POLITICS OF RACE

Near McKeesrock, Pa., a steelworker expressed a typical comment when he declared angrily, "The only good thing Goldwater ever did was to vote against civil rights. But we're not going to give up everything we've fought for, like our unions and Social Security."

A San Francisco fireman talked approvingly of Goldwater's "not wanting to give Negroes anything for nothing," but concluded, "I'm a laboring man and Goldwater is not for me."

In Bell Gardens, a comparatively low-income suburb of Los Angeles, a factory foreman praised Goldwater for "standing up" against the civil rights law and agreed "we need a showdown in Viet Nam."

Still he was staying with Johnson.

"Goldwater's got all us old people scared," he explained. "I'm 62 and the old lady is 60. We don't want some screwball coming in and upsetting this Social Security business. I might have voted for the sucker but for that."

Goldwater, in short, had threatened the Democratic coalition on too many different points to crack it apart. Each new front of attack he opened up united another segment of the electorate behind the Democratic banner.

Much the same conflict between racial angers and the fears Goldwater stirred raged in the South as well. Here, as well, when I returned for a second interviewing swing in October I found a sizable shift toward Johnson underway.

Talk of a realignment of both parties so strong in the summer had been shed with autumn's leaves. Only in the racially sensitive areas were Goldwater supporters determined to protest aloud their personal convictions.

The general expectation that Johnson would win stirred much speculation of what actions he might take against those Southern states that did not support him. In North Carolina the fear talk was that "he'll cut out subsidies for tobacco farmers"; in Florida and Virginia that "we'll lose our military bases if Goldwater carries our state." A real estate broker in Richmond contended, "We have to be realistic. If Virginia goes for Goldwater and Johnson wins big, the Johnson crowd is likely to shut down some of Virginia's military installations."

The Democratic campaigners drilled away like dentists at these and other fears. One TV spot which hammered at the idea that Goldwater would "take away Social Security" showed a Social Security card being torn in two. This spot got talked about and was even distorted.

A laundry worker in Greensboro remarked, "I was all set to vote for Goldwater until I heard he threw a Social Security card down on the floor and stamped on it."

Goldwater had denied being against Social Security and had actually voted for higher Social Security payments, but this action was overshadowed by his opposition to Medicare.

In St. Petersburg, one former Long Island resident shook with anger as she declared, "Goldwater thinks we're all rich enough to live without Social Security or Medicare. My husband just had his eyes operated on. What do you think he paid for a pair of eyeglasses? A hundred and forty-eight dollars! How far does a pension go on that?"

In the two St. Petersburg neighborhoods I visited it was easy to see why there would be no way of checking this feeling that "Goldwater is against old people" once such talk began. Through that whole day of interviewing not a child was ever in sight. On the streets there were only old people to exchange "how are you today?" with other old people, and to talk of their fears that Social Security might be cut off and their hopes that Medicare would pay their medical bills.

Usually St. Petersburg gives the Republicans a 50,000 plurality in presidential elections. In 1964 it actually went for Johnson by 18,000 votes. This difference was enough to swing Florida to the Democrats.

The Republican Dilemma

Shortly before President Kennedy's assassination, in a talk at Oberlin College, I ventured the judgment that the Republican party was on the verge of making a historic, all-out bid for the political support of the South.

In view of the Goldwater disaster one might expect the GOP to take solemn vows against another Southern venture.

But the political pressures compelling the Republicans to look Southward remain quite strong; they may even be intensifying despite Goldwater's showing.

The basic fact is that the South has been the only part of the nation where the Republicans have gained political strength since the end of World War II. Between 1950 and 1962, for example, the Republicans increased their Southern seats in Congress from two to eleven. In 1964 the number jumped to sixteen despite the loss of two Texas districts which the Republicans had held earlier.

In the voting for President from 1932 through 1948 the GOP had not drawn more than a fourth of the South's vote.

Eisenhower lifted this to 37 percent in 1952 and 49 percent in 1956. Nixon in 1960 drew 46 percent of the total vote cast in the eleven secession states. Goldwater drew 49 percent of the vote.

Between the Eisenhower and Goldwater elections a marked shift took place in the type of Southerners who voted Republican. For the future the real Republican choice in political strategy will not be whether to woo or shun the South but which part of the South to bid for — the Eisenhower South or Goldwater South?

This choice, in turn, should be viewed as part of the process by which the Republican party is being transformed from a strictly Northern affair to a national party with strength in every part of the nation.

Eisenhower's 1952 victory was popularly attributed to his personality and war-hero fame. In the South, though, his support was really a projection of the tendency toward economic voting which began with Roosevelt's New Deal. Being bound to a Democratic tradition, the South was slower to realign than the rest of the nation. Some evidences of this new voting cleavage on income lines show up in the South in 1944 and 1948, but the real breakthrough came in 1952.

It was in the cities of the South that Eisenhower — and Nixon's vote followed much the same pattern — drew his strongest support. In all of these cities it was always the better-income neighborhoods that gave Eisenhower their heaviest vote.

In rural counties the Eisenhower strength was concentrated mainly in the towns, among Main Street merchants.

The farmers themselves, much as in the North, tended to stick with the Democratic party.

The 1962 balloting showed a tendency for this economic voting to be projected into state and Congressional elections. All eleven Congressional seats won by the GOP in 1962 were districts that Eisenhower had carried.

In Texas the 46 percent of the vote registered by Jack Cox represented the best showing of any Republican candidate for governor in recent Texas history. Although he fell nine percentage points below Eisenhower's showing and three percentage points under Nixon's 1960 vote, still the support for Cox flowed along in precisely the same channels that were first grooved out by Eisenhower.

A sampling of rural Texas communities showed that Cox ran nearly 10 percent stronger among the Main Street merchants than among the farmers in the countryside. Inside the Texas cities his vote followed the same scaling by income as in the 1952-1960 presidential voting.

Where Houston's well-to-do River Oaks section gave Cox 79 percent of its vote, worker precincts dropped him below 35 percent.

Of the 140 Houston precincts carried by Cox all but four voted Republican for President in 1952, 1956 and 1960. The four exceptions narrowly missed giving Nixon a majority.

In 1956 the Eisenhower-Stevenson vote divided fifty-fifty in precincts where homes were valued around $10,000. The break-even point for Cox in 1962 came in neighborhoods where the average home valuation was around $13,000.

In both Tulsa and Oklahoma City the same pattern prevailed. The victorious Republican candidate for governor, Henry Bellmon, carried almost the identical precincts won by Eisenhower and Nixon.

In sum, the 1952-62 decade had brought a considerable degree of political realignment to the South, with old one-party loyalties giving way to a new voting division based largely on economic interest. This realignment, however, had never been completed because of the unresolved racial struggle.

In nearly every Southern state racial emotions were — and still are — sufficiently powerful to constitute the balance of voting power. When these racial feelings lie bedded down, the political balance favors the Democrats. But a popular recoil against efforts to enforce desegregation could swing much of the South out of the Democratic fold.

In Alabama the Republican vote for U. S. Senator in 1962 hit a new Republican high because of the angers stirred by Kennedy's use of federal troops at the Universities of Mississippi and Alabama. The three urban counties containing Birmingham, Mobile and Montgomery voted 56 percent Republican compared with 52 percent for Nixon and 46 and 50 percent for Eisenhower in 1952 and 1956. Worker precincts in Birmingham, Mobile and Montgomery that had gone for Kennedy two to one swung to give the Republicans a majority.

Even more explosive was the reaction of the black-belt counties, which are most sensitive to the racial issue. In ten Alabama counties Negroes outnumbered the whites, but the Negroes living in these counties were not permitted to vote.

These ten so-called black-belt counties gave Eisenhower a third of their vote. They went 54 percent Republican in the 1962 election for Senator.

When, after the 1963 Birmingham demonstrations, Democratic defections threatened in the Northern cities, some Republican strategists thought the time had come for an all-out assault upon the South. The political stage seemed set for an effort to merge into a conservative coalition all the issues symbolic of resistance to "too much government."

If he had been able to hold the Eisenhower economic vote, Goldwater might have ridden the racial surge to sweep the South. As it was, he succeeded only in changing the racial-economic mix of the Republican vote.

Where Eisenhower drew 54 percent of the vote in the major Southern cities, Goldwater dropped to 48 percent. In the most racially sensitive counties, Eisenhower drew only 42 percent of the vote but Goldwater jumped to 62 percent.

This shift in the racial-economic mix becomes even sharper if the cities of the Deep South are separated from those in the less racially sensitive South. In the major cities of Alabama, Georgia, Louisiana and Mississippi, Goldwater drew 60 percent of the vote, but only 42 percent in the cities of North Carolina, Tennessee, Texas, Virginia and Florida.

The Johnson landslide, it should be noted, did not erase the pattern of economic voting, but only weakened it. A sampling of higher income precincts in Florida, Virginia, Texas and North Carolina showed 59 percent for Goldwater, while worker precincts in the same states gave him only 38 percent.

Compared with 1960, these better-income precincts were

10 percent less Republican in 1964. The worker precincts were 14 percent less Republican.

The significance of this racial-economic split emerges more sharply when one compares the vote in the South with what happened in the rest of the country. One then sees how considerable has been the progress made in recent years in unifying the South with the rest of the nation. All of the more urbanized Southern states responded to the same influences that swept the North, the West and even the Border states. Only the Deep South voted to stay apart.

The 1964 voting returns read like a summing up communique of how the second Civil War has fared. Turn back to that earlier chapter and see how the split in Southern feeling described in my surveys corresponds to the 1964 vote. In the six states where desegregation was accepted, Johnson won. The five Deep South states which Goldwater won were the states where the desegregation battle still raged.

The election outcome, in short, suggests that progress in achieving racial unity strengthens the Democratic cause. Delays in enforcing desegregation hurt the Democrats.

The whole drama of party realignment in the South has been something of a race against time, a race in which the Democrats have striven consciously or unconsciously to reduce the political weight of racial anger so that economic and other issues would finally emerge as decisive.

In the long run, it is my feeling that the Republicans as well will find it wiser to follow the Eisenhower pattern of pitching their main appeal in the South to economics rather than race. But this will not be accomplished easily. Even, if this is done, the issue of "What strategy for the South" will aggravate the conflict between varied Republican factions in the North and Southwest over which direction the GOP should follow nationally. This struggle, in turn, could split and weaken the Republicans nationally, as happened in 1964.

One strong reason why the political battling in the South divides the Republicans nationally is the fact that GOP political needs vary so drastically in the North and the South.

To crack the South the Republicans must sharpen rather than blur political issues. After all, why should a Southern Democrat break loose from tradition unless a quite marked difference is posed in what the Democrats and Republicans stand for?

But in many Northern states, the Republicans would prefer to blur and dull the edge of party differences. The fact that so much of the Northern Democratic following has climbed to tax-paying, middle-class status has brought into being a new, moderate-minded generation of voters, who are neither fully comfortable with all of the old Roosevelt slogans nor prepared to embrace Republicanism either. That these voters can be won over by a strategy of blurring the differences between the parties can be seen in the election of such Republican governors as Nelson Rockefeller in New York, William Scranton in Pennsylvania, and George Romney in Michigan; also in the popularity of Senators like Thomas Kuchel in California, Jacob Javits in New York and Clifford Case in New Jersey.

The Republican ordeal, in other words, is really a two-in-one agony. First there is the issue whether to sharpen or blur, to use the hammer or the glove. Then, as far as the South is concerned, which conflict should be sharpened, economic issues or racial angers?

Those choices are almost certain to be one of the more critical issues in the struggle for the GOP presidential nomination in 1968. Which way the GOP turns is likely to be shaped by actual events — whether we are at war or peace and how high or low is the level of the economy — and by what the 1966 elections reveal as to which discontents exert the strongest appeals to the voters.

The course any party takes is determined largely by the voters who are attracted to that party. One danger that threatens the "liberal" Republicans is that they must run for re-election in strongly Democratic areas. Should the Democrats manage to hold the full Johnson vote in the industrial East, the liberal Republicans could be defeated, even while more conservative Republicans emerged as winners in less Democratic states.

The political attraction exerted by the South will lessen if GOP candidates in the North crack a good part of the Negro vote. If there is no Negro break then the value of the South will rise in the calculations of Republican strategists.

Which part of the Southern electorate exerts the strongest lure is likely to be determined by where the fires of insurgency flame highest, by who in the South will want to use the Republican party as a means of protesting against Washington.

Some Deep South politicians who have turned Republican, like Senator Strom Thurmond and Congressman Albert Watson in South Carolina, will be working with the Goldwater Republicans and John Birch Society to channel GOP strategy into another Goldwater-kind of bid to turn back the racial clock.

Still, another open anti-Negro appeal isn't too likely. The next real test of the politics of race will come, I suspect, in a more subtle form.

Through the whole South the desegregation struggle has left in its wake a desire for political reprisal or protest against "that crowd in Washington." With some Southerners that sentiment is sufficiently intense so that they have turned Republican. With many more, their Democratic loyalty has been weakened rather than broken.

If other issues began troubling people — if the economy were to falter or we suffered heavy casualties and a serious setback abroad — then these weakened loyalties could snap. The turn in the South would be quickened and strengthed by the smoldering desire for political revenge.

The Negro Dilemma

As for the Negroes, theirs is a somewhat paradoxical situation.

Since Eisenhower's intervention at Little Rock, the Negro strategy for forcing racial change in the South has been built around executive action, on the belief that the President will intervene with troops if necessary in any showdown.

This strategy places a high premium on voting allegiance to the Democratic party, which has gained Negro leaders an enormous influence with Democratic Presidents.

In voting for Congress, however, this same Negro Democratic solidarity has had a somewhat boomerang effect. It has contributed to Southern dominance in the committees of Congress and served, also, as a major pressure pushing the Republicans toward alliance with the white South.

Consider the change in Congressional representation in the twelve largest cities in the nation. Since 1930 the Northward migration of Negroes from the South has more than tripled the Negro population in these twelve cities. This has had a double impact.

First, whole sections of the inner city have been converted into a virtually solid Negro core. By 1962 five of these cities were sending Negro congressmen, all Democrats, to Washington.

Second, as more and more Negroes have moved into the center of cities, white families have been pushed out. Most of these families have been Democrats. As they spread through the cities and into the suburbs, they have toppled strongly Republican districts, even where Negroes do not live.

These twelve cities combined with their suburbs contain just under a fourth of all the seats in Congress. Between 1952, when the Republicans last held control of Congress, and 1964 the Republican share of these urban and suburban seats has dropped from 54 to 32.

Six of these twelve cities — St. Louis, Baltimore, Detroit, Milwaukee, Philadelphia and Boston — have been without a single Republican congressman for some years.

Largely as a result of these urban losses it has become virtually impossible for the Republicans to recapture control of Congress — unless they can pick up additional seats in the South.

Of the 295 seats held by the Democrats, after the 1964 vote, 172 have been Democratic since at least 1948. Another 36 can be considered "safe" because of population changes and one sided Democratic pluralities.

This adds up to 208 rigidly Democratic seats, just 10 short of a clear majority.

Only 77 of the 140 seats now held by the Republicans can be considered "safe."

To gain control of Congress, the Republicans would have to win nearly all of the 150 seats where there is some contest — something that isn't likely to happen unless there is a catastrophic depression or the meaning attached to both parties changes drastically.

Johnson's 1964 landslide swept in enough new Democratic congressmen to break up the old coalition of Northern Republicans and Southern Democrats. Succeeding elections are likely to shift the relative party strengths, with the Republicans remaining in the minority. In that position the Republicans will find themselves constantly tempted to enter into coalition with some Democratic faction. In the legislative process the interests of Negroes, if they remain solidly Democratic, are likely to be traded off for Southern support on issues of importance to Republican constituencies.

This danger of too strong a commitment to one party has been recognized by many Negro leaders and scholars who, like Gunnar Myrdal, have urged Negroes to adopt a flexible strategy of dividing between both major parties. But this is not easily done. The main difficulty lies with the Negro's economic and social makeup, which makes it difficult for him to divide politically.

The contrast with the white South is significant. Among white Southerners one finds quite a wide range of economic interests, so wide that it has become difficult, if not impossible, to encompass them all in one party. The normal division on economic lines yields enough of a Republican vote so that only a moderate degree of additional dissatisfaction is needed to swing some Southern states.

Among Negroes, however, one still finds comparatively little economic differentiation.

Trade union solidarity is far stronger among Negro than white workers. In 1958 when right-to-work proposals were voted on in four states — Ohio, California, Colorado and Kansas — Negroes went nine to one against them, by far the heaviest opposition shown by any worker group.

Higher income Negro neighborhoods do show something more of a Republican vote than do worker areas. But, on the whole, the makeup of the new Negro middle class in the Northern cities tends to knit the Negro more firmly to the Democratic party.

In numerical strength, government workers constitute by far the largest single element in this middle class. The federal government actually employs one in every eighteen Negro workers. Of 300,000 Negroes who worked for Uncle Sam in 1962, more than 1,400 held jobs which paid over $10,000 a year. Another 34,143 held jobs paying between $5,000 and $10,000 a year.

Perhaps as important, the sense of common interest with "business" or "management" which pulls so many other voters to the Republicans is extremely low among Negroes.

Even among the best educated Negroes, few envision careers with a large company. The Negro financial stake in business is quite limited.

Of the 100 Negroes rated as most influential by *Ebony* magazine in 1963, only nine were clearly identifiable as businessmen. One, Jackie Robinson, is vice-president of a restaurant chain; another, S. S. Fuller, is a cosmetics manufacturer who has successfully competed in the white market.

The seven other influential Negro businessmen were in insurance and savings-and-loan companies, catering primarily to Negro customers. While Negro wealth has been growing, the few Negro businesses of any size remain primarily life insurance companies.

In looking at other middle-class elements one finds sizable numbers of ministers and teachers, but in 1955 the annual increase of Negro graduate engineers stood at only 150; the yearly crop of additional doctors and lawyers was around 200.

These differences between the Negro middle class and the middle class developed by other "minority" groups are highly significant. They should give us a keener understanding of what the word "progress" really means. Many people think of the climb out of poverty in statistical terms, as if the level of family income is the sensitive measure to watch. But this overlooks the fact that the future of every minority group is also shaped by *how* it climbs, by which pursuits are open to the members of that group and which remain closed, by the diversity or narrowness of their educational attainments and the structure of their economic interests.

These characteristics, in turn, shape the kind of political role that the minority group is capable of playing.

As presently constituted, the Negro middle class is still too precarious and dependent upon government for Negroes to exercise genuine political independence. The Negro middle class lacks the qualities of restful confidence; it cannot risk much of a break in its voting solidarity. Temporary bolts may take place as in 1956, but the basic Democratic loyalty of the Negro voter in the Northern states is not likely to be shattered, not even by an impassioned sense of racialism.

Dependent bargaining inside the Democratic coalition is likely to dominate the Negro's political role through the immediate years ahead. The political problem posed by the Negroes is likely to remain primarily what impact they will have on white voters. What will the Democratic leaders have to do to appease or satisfy Negro demands? How will white voters react to these actions?

The continuing political pressures exerted by the Negroes will prove constructive if they force the Democratic leaders into actions and policies which contribute to racial unity through the nation. But these pressures could also prove disruptive.

While one cannot anticipate the many ways in which this impact will be felt, we can be sure that it will be felt through the whole of our society, beyond the racial front alone. In fact, the more difficult it becomes to quiet racial tensions, the more attention Democratic leaders are likely to give to bolstering the nonracial ties that hold the Negroes and whites in the Democratic party.

President Johnson's heavy emphasis on Medicare in the 1964 campaign was motivated largely by the search for appeals that would divide and overcome the racial anti-pathies of lower income whites in the South and North.

In Olympia, S.C., a widow who had voted for Nixon in 60 was shifting to Johnson because "Goldwater wouldn't never sign that law to pay our hospital bills."

Early in the 1964 campaign I often ran into voters who would start by saying, "I'm voting for the feller against the nigger," but would then shift to say, "I'll stick with Johnson" when asked, "What if Johnson comes out strong for Medicare for older people and Goldwater votes against it?"

Negroes will remain a powerful force for additional gov-ernment spending in many other ways as well. The prevalence of so many poorly educated, jobless Negroes will act as a heavy pressure for greater efforts in the field of education and, probably, make-work employment.

A high proportion of Negroes are dependent on govern-ment assistance in some form. Perhaps the only way of easing the problems of the larger cities may be through liberal finan-cial transfusions from the federal government.

One prime objective of the new Department of Urban Affairs is to serve as a claimant agency for direct grants from the federal government to the cities, bypassing the state gov-ernments. The antipoverty program has been another effort at accomplishing this same aim.

But other Democratic voters have been much more divided than the Negroes on the merits of spending. In the past these Democrats have tended to favor government spending up to the level where it holds up employment, but they have been inclined to balk against spending when it meant higher taxes or inflationary price rises.

This conflict over spending is likely to have its heaviest impact on state and local politics. During recent years, while federal taxes have been lowered, local taxes have risen drastically as states and cities have been forced to provide schools, hospitals and other services for a rising and shifting population.

The taxpayer revolts that have broken out in many communities help explain why so many governors have been defeated for re-election in recent years. These taxpayer resentments tend also to be sharpened by the racial crisis. To improve the schooling of Negroes and ease their other problems, extra funds must be raised and spent.

As part of this urban struggle, increased recognition will undoubtedly be given the Negro in the big city machines. In New York City, a Negro, J. Raymond Jones, has been named to head Tammany Hall. Other patronage favors will be extended as a means of strengthening the faithful Negro Democrats against the more militant Negroes outside of the machines.

But such a strategy could backfire somewhat. In Philadelphia the new job preferences given Negroes angered even the staunchest party workers in white neighborhoods. Back in 1959 there were 33 precincts which voted 90 percent Democratic for mayor. In the 1963 mayor's election the Negro precincts in this group voted 85 percent Democratic, but the white precincts broke to only 65 percent Democrati .

Negro-white tensions will also be an important, perhaps decisive force in the rivalry over who is to control the Democratic party. Probably the weight of Negro influence will strengthen the political hands of Robert and Edward Kennedy against Hubert Humphrey or any other Johnson choice.

East of the Mississippi, most Northern cities are fairly heavily Catholic and it is in Catholic neighborhoods that one finds the strongest resentments against Negroes. One's ability to reduce possible Catholic defections on race is likely to be one consideration in naming the Democratic presidential candidate.

Also one should not underestimate the strength of the Negro's emotional attachment to the memory of President Kennedy. No group of voters in the nation felt his assassination so deep a personal loss.

"Kennedy really fought for us," and "it was like having a member of the family die" were common remarks made by Negroes right after the assassination.

A fifty-eight-year-old mechanic in Brooklyn said, "Kennedy's picture is on my wall. It hurts me to look at it now." He went on, "I'm a Democrat, but I won't vote for any Southerner."

When I raised the possibility of Robert Kennedy as Johnson's Vice-President, the mechanic replied, "That's different. I'd go for Robert. He's a fine man."

A chauffeur in Pittsburgh, when asked about a Johnson-Kennedy ticket replied, "I'd vote for it once in the morning and once at night."

How shall we sum up what we have learned about the politics of race?

Two conclusions stand out:

First, for some years to come the Negro is likely to remain a restless, disturbing force politically.

The long-run fate of the Democratic party — the issue of survival or slow death — hinges on whether it will be able to unify the nation racially, which really means unifying both the South and the Negroes with the rest of the nation. As we have seen, the first such effort, to project the Negro-labor alliance into the South, failed. Instead the South responded with a double insurgency: 1) an economic revolt aimed at checking government spending and the power of labor unions and (2) a racial reaction designed to counter the influence of Negro voting in the North.

This failure to remake the South in the image of Northern liberalism, spurred the rise of a new militancy on the part of the Southern Negro, a militancy unrestrained by the compromises of coalition politics. This militancy, in turn, transferred to the Northern Negro, threatens to alienate many white Democratic voters in the big cities.

One of two doors can be opened to the future. Unrelenting pressures by the Negroes may force the Democrats to rise to the necessity of framing a program of racial unification for the nation, or the Democrats will fail in this effort. In that case the nation will suffer the throes and agonies that come with the slow deterioration of the majority party.

The second conclusion that arises from this analysis of the politics of race is that too heavy a reliance has been placed on Negro voting.

The absence of voting rights is intolerable. As the South has shown, a minimum voting representation is indispensable to avoid being disregarded completely. But it does not follow that the bargaining power of the Negro will rise proportionately with each fresh increase in Negro voting numbers.

As more and more Negroes exercise the right of suffrage, and if they continue to vote as a bloc, white voters can be expected to unite against them. If political power is to be the deciding force, enough white resistance can be expected to check Negro advances to limits acceptable to whites.

But perhaps more important, the distorted weight of attention that has been given Negro voting is producing a Negro political power that is far greater than his attainments in education, or economically. If this persists the Negro's political role cannot prove constructive. Up to a point the Negro can look to government and politics to gain him the rights he has been denied. But for these gains to be lasting — and unifying — the Negro must be able to keep those rights and gains through his own efforts.

Unless this can be done the politics of race in the future will reduce itself to a single question — how much will it take to buy off the Negro so he doesn't make too much trouble?

The task is primarily one for whites. Negroes can be excused the emphasis they have put on political power because they have had so little choice. But for white voters the moral is quite another matter. Many "liberals" have deceived themselves with the belief that as Negroes gained political strength they would be able to demand and get better treatment. This belief encouraged the thought that all of these problems would be easier to deal with in the future than today.

But time is no such ally of ours. The Negro is not strong enough to force the white man to do the right thing. The greater the political power acquired by the Negro the more insistent will become the need to look beyond the ballot box and bring into existence the conditions which will enable Negroes to hold their rights on their own abilities and not by looking to the government.

Can we devise such a program? The evidence to date still testifies "No."

9

Toward Racial Peace

"A New Approach"

At varied points in this book the term "war" has been used to describe our racial crisis. Many readers have probably read it as a mere figure of speech. Yet, in sad truth, we have been like two warring nations on this issue; not alone in the clash of the federal and Southern state governments but in the determination of so many whites to stay separate from the Negro.

It is time we started thinking of how to make racial peace among ourselves, of how to become one nation again. Throughout the past century we have allowed racial relations to shape themselves around two pressures — where the white man resisted least and where the Negro pressed hardest.

To continue to bargain the Negro's militancy against the white man's resistance is an invitation to tragedy. It will yield a distortion of progress, with a lopsided political power unsupported by other gains. Racial advances will remain largely token and illusory because they have not been accompanied by crucial structural changes. Even as the walls of segregation are tumbled, we are likely to find that new walls of embittered racialism have risen to keep us divided in a different way.

189

What is needed, I believe, is a consciously thought through drive for racial unification. Each of us — white and black — should ask ourselves what conditions of thinking and living are necessary before we can be united racially.

Having defined what needs to be done, we should strive to guide the raging conflict so it helps bring into being these changed conditions that would make racial peace realizable in the future.

Certainly we will differ among ourselves in defining the requirements of racial unity. Every year or two we may also have to change our definition somewhat, reflecting what we have learned. Still, some such conscious, directed effort will serve the nation better than to assume that racial progress is automatic or to let the future be shaped by the Negro's probing for the weak spots in the white man's resistance.

What are the conditions that are needed for racial peace to become attainable?

The key requirement, I believe, is to replace racialism with individualism.

Equality, in its strictly literal sense, is impossible, of course. We are born with such varying blood chemistries and talents of nervousness that none of us is truly equal to another. We run, walk, work, think, eat at different tempos.

What is indispensable is:

First, that each person stand equal before the law, with the same chance to advance himself on the basis of his competitive abilities.

Second, that we restructure our own thinking to be able to treat each Negro as a recognizable individual and not as an anonymous black face.

Putting this commitment to individualism into effect will be prodigiously difficult. Also, quite different actions will be required in the North and in the South.

In the South the first need has long been to end all racial discrimination by law. Any segregation ordinances that are still left should be repealed or declared unconstitutional. All taboos of "white only" and "colored only" should come tumbling down.

Until that comes to pass the social framework for orderly, evolutionary racial progress will be missing. As long as the taboos of white supremacy remain in force, they tend to require white Southerners to treat all Negroes as if they were alike. Southerners must be freed of this compulsion; they must be free to draw a distinction between one Negro and another.

Individuals may continue to fear, hate or shun the Negro, but that should be their own private affair and not be enforced or institutionalized by law. A barber's wife in Greensboro expressed the distinction to be drawn when she said, "I don't believe in intermarriage, but I can teach my children to avoid that. We don't have to keep abusing the colored people to prevent that."

While the 1964 civil rights law was being discussed in Congress, I advanced one suggestion which I hoped would speed an end to all discrimination by law in the South. My proposal called for the President naming a Racial Peace Commission for each Southern state. Each commission was to be charged with the task of drafting a specific program, setting forth in precise detail what further desegregation steps would be taken voluntarily by that state over the next three to four years.

The emphasis was to be on "voluntary action" — giving each state the opportunity to demonstrate what it was prepared to do on its own toward ending racial discrimination, without marshals, without troops, without court orders, without violence, without demonstrations, without "outside agitators."

This appeal for "voluntary" action seemed worth making for one main reason — to try to end the psychological war that has been raging in the minds of so many Southerners. Wherever desegregation has taken place in the South, we have seen, it has weakened the opposition to further desegregation. The actual changes in racial relations have been less troubling to white Southerners than the mental war they have been waging to prevent change.

"Voluntary" action, if it were possible, could remove the feeling that these changes are being forced on the South by hostile Northerners. Without that external enemy to provide the unifying tensions, I doubted that the cause of segregation could be held together.

The passage of the civil rights law has given partial effect to some of these proposals. The law creates a new Community Relations Service, which, while different from a Racial Peace Commission, does establish a bargaining agency through which racial adjustments can be worked into detailed, orderly programs.

More important, the decisive nature of Goldwater's defeat has brought a significant change in the mood of the Southerners.

While the Selma demonstrations were in the headlines I

made an interviewing swing through six Southern states. In every state I found a greater readiness to accept further desegregation than at any time since the Supreme Court's decision of 1954.

"We've got to take it" or "You can't fight the federal government" was the general refrain sounded in every Southern city and small town where I interviewed.

Often these comments were accompanied by profane declarations such as, "I'm not a Democrat anymore" or "It hurts like sin having things crammed down your throat." Still not a single Southerner interviewed voiced open defiance of the law.

On all my previous Southern surveys, there always were some men or women who declared, "Let's close down our schools and make the government open them" or "I'll burn down my motel" before accepting a Negro customer.

This new mood of acceptance reflected a general feeling that the desegregation battle had been fought and the Deep South had lost.

To most Southerners the 1964 election was the equivalent of a racial referendum, in which the issue had been posed bluntly and sharply without any blurring similarity in the positions of the two parties. What the voting returns showed was clear. A South Carolina grocer, who had voted for Goldwater said, "It doesn't matter what I think. When the whole country is for it we might as well get used to it."

I also found that acceptance of the new civil rights law had been eased by the fact that relatively few Negroes have taken advantage of its provisions. This prompted many whites to reason, "all the Negroes want is to know they can do these things."

Other Southerners have learned to look away from what troubles them. In Raleigh, a produce worker's wife explained, "I never ask a motel whether they accept colored people. If I knew they did I wouldn't be able to sleep thinking some Negro had been in that bed. So I just don't ask questions."

Others, though, said, "I've stopped eating in restaurants" or "I don't go to the movies any more."

The wife of an insurance agent in Raleigh remarked, "At first I was startled to see white and colored eating together. Now I just take it for granted."

Some Southerners are beginning to draw a distinction between "cutthroat niggers" and those "who want to improve themselves." Several mothers volunteered, "It's all right to go to school with colored children who are trying to advance themselves."

In Columbia, S.C., an electrician's wife recalled, "We had car trouble and a colored person stopped on the road and offered to help. Later I asked Bill if he would have stopped to help a stranger at night. He replied, 'I don't know.' All we can think of is the meanness of Nigras. But there's good in them."

In another striking change from the old days of monolithic anti-Negro solidarity, I found that husbands and wives would often disagree with one another while being interviewed. In North Carolina an insurance collector's wife burst out, "George Wallace should be tarred and feathered!"

Her husband retorted, "Martin Luther King ought to be."

A machinist's wife in Richmond felt, "You've got to bring the Nigras forward. My husband doesn't want to change but he's wrong. The Nigra situation has gone too far to hold them back. It would lead to a war among the races."

In some of the touchiest states, like Mississippi, Georgia and South Carolina, leaders of business and government were working to strengthen the public's acceptance of racial change. The employment provisions of the civil rights law would soon be taking effect, and many Southern employers were trying to prepare the way for its acceptance. Violence, it was being argued, hurts a state economically. Continued progress requires recognizing that the South is "a part of the Union" and "bound by the civil rights law."

One should not leap upon these developments as evidence that the desegregation war in the South is over. However, these comments do point the direction toward which Southern feeling is moving. They do show that Goldwater's defeat reconciled many Southerners to a stepped up pace of racial change.

At least two disquieting factors remain however.

First, often when people are defeated in a bitter emotional struggle, a desire for political reprisal and even political revenge hangs on. Many Southerners, even while conceding, "It has to come" want to cast some kind of protest vote against "that crowd in Washington."

In this sense I wondered how wise or useful a move was the March from Selma to Montgomery. Many white Southerners who thought "Negroes should get this voting law" felt "this March is no way to go about it."

What seemed to rankle Southerners most deeply was a feeling that the March was so open a display of Negro and federal political power and of their own impotence.

"I feel so helpless I just don't want to talk about it," snapped one salesman in Jackson, Miss.

"Negroes are going to get their voting law," complained a factory worker in Richmond. "This March is just rubbing salt in wounds."

In Atlanta a truck driver conceded, "the Negro is getting his rights and I guess there will be room for both of us." But then this truck driver remarked bitterly, "You don't need states any more. All you need is the Supreme Court and a helper."

It was to Alabama's Governor Wallace that the angrier Southerners turned for consolation. On one street corner in Clanton, Ala., a well-dressed merchant was getting obvious pleasure in telling several friends how "Wallace slickered Johnson into making the federal government pay the cost of guarding that March.

Not only in towns and cities in Alabama, but in Atlanta, Richmond, Memphis, Raleigh and Jackson men and women being interviewed asked me, "Did you hear Wallace's last speech?" or, "What did you think of his point that he would obey the federal courts but that King would not?"

Often people said, " I wish we had a governor like George Wallace to lead us."

A second factor clouding the future is the fact that in much of the South one can still expect only token compliance with the civil rights law and the Supreme Court's decisions.

An argument that broke out in one Atlanta family while it was being interviewed was revealing. We were talking of whether it was better to start school integration with the youngest or the oldest children.

"Begin with the youngest," contended the middle-aged wife of a building trades worker. "Little children don't have prejudices. They won't say mean things to each other. They don't know the difference."

"That's the trouble," interrupted her married daughter. "You should start with high school kids who know the difference and won't mix. If they play together as kids, the girls will get to like the Negro boys. They'll grow up and intermarry."

That argument, which has been repeated to me in every Southern city, bares the two conflicting pulls that divide the emotions of most Southerners.

While some think of a gradual shedding of racial prejudices and a steady evolution toward racial equality, others dread any coming together of the two races. For them the higher the walls of tension that separate the races the better.

How can the racial conflict be guided so it strengthens the hands of those who would shed racial hatred and weakens those Southerners who would keep the barriers high between the two races?

No simple formula can be advanced but a few thoughts might be worth suggesting.

First, delay in pressing the cause of integration and enforcing the Supreme Court's decision would hurt rather than help. Wherever desegregation has taken place it has made the

next step easier. Whatever is left of the structure of segregation in the South should be pulled down quickly; the faster it
is done, the sooner the conflict will be resolved.

Psychologically there would be great advantages if this
could be done voluntarily by the South itself. Racial Peace
Commissions or their equivalent could speed the adjustments
and leave behind less of a desire for political revenge. But if
the choice is between action by the federal government or little or nothing being done, then action is the wiser course.

This seems the direction toward which Washington has
been moving. School boards through the South have been
threatened with the loss of all federal funds unless they sign
compliance pledges to do some mixing of colored and white
children. In the first response, about a sixth of the school districts balked at such pledges, while another fourth signed
somewhat doubtful pledges. But more than half indicated
they would comply.

In four Alabama school districts which I checked, the majority of persons interviewed supported their school board
signing a compliance pledge even though "we don't like it."
A factory worker in Calera summed up this general feeling
when he said, "We can't pay our teachers the salaries they
want now. What can we do without federal money? We'd
have to close our schools."

Still miracles of compliance cannot be expected, particularly in the more rural areas. It may seem simple enough for
agents of the federal government to demand action in any
town. But what happens when the agent — and the government — takes the highway out of town? Will the Negroes in

that community have the stamina and bargaining power to hold those gains? Will the climate of opinion favor or obstruct their advance?

In battling out the answers to those questions, we must expect that many Negroes will prefer to move North rather than continue the battle.

Those Negroes who stay can probably count on some improvement in their economic lot. But for many Negroes these economic gains are likely to prove much smaller than needed.

In farming — and 40 percent of the South's Negroes still live in rural areas — little future for the Southern Negro is seen by most Agriculture Department experts. The number of Negro landowners has been shrinking rapidly; those who remain are chiefly older farmers on subsistence-size acreages. Negro farmers have also lagged behind white farmers in expanding the size of their farms and in shifting from cotton to dairying or cattle raising or specialty crops. They have lacked the capital to make these shifts; also the skills. Thus, as Marcus Garvey would have pointed out, they have been black farmers in a countryside controlled by the white man.

In Georgia one enterprising Negro farmer, who had saved some money from an off-the-farm job, moved into peach growing. When he did, as the story was told to Calvin Beale of the U. S. Department of Agriculture, the Negro got telephone calls from white persons saying, "Peach growing is a white man's job."

The local peach growers' cooperative refused to handle his peaches. The Negro finally had to sell some of his land to pay off his losses.

In factory employment some racial progress has been made
— new factories in parts of South Carolina have been opened
on a desegregated basis with community approval, not resistance — and the new civil rights law will be helpful.

More Negro workers will be put on if employers can say,
"It's the law. I have to do it." Even at best, though, it is doubtful that the increased job opportunities for Negroes will be
adequate, particularly for those leaving high school and college.

Continued migration out of the South seems likely, and
continued migration means more racial trouble in the North.

The Northern Dilemma

Outside of the South it may prove even more difficult to put
into effect a commitment to individualism.

In the North and West there are no laws that discriminate
against Negroes. Some legislation even tends to favor them.
Still most of us have shown slight ability to distinguish between individual Negroes. We continue to react to them in
terms of mass stereotypes.

The indispensable action that is needed is to give the Negroes residential mobility, to enable them to disperse and
move freely in their search for living quarters. White resistance has been most intense, of course, on this housing front.
But without this mobility the conditions for racial peace in
the North cannot be brought into being.

To the degree that Negroes remain walled into black-belt
ghettos, to that degree they will remain a separate, subnation in this country.

If individualism is to replace racialism in Negro feeling, individual Negro families must be able to register their social and economic progress by moving to better neighborhoods. They need to be able to separate themselves and their children from slum conditions, from the gangs of delinquents, street-corner prostitutes, narcotic addicts, and other transients who turn some city streets into a jungle.

Among one-time immigrant groups in the past this drive to climb the social ladder, to move into a "nicer" neighborhood, served as perhaps the strongest single spur to achievement. It organized the aspirations and energies of these immigrant families — giving their savings a value far beyond the interest rates paid by banks.

The spread of such a sense of climbing purpose would be felt in every aspect of Negro living; it would reduce the tendency to look to government for advancement and heighten pride in individual achievement.

The Negro needs also to be able to move more freely so that white people can learn to differentiate between various kinds of Negroes. Currently our thinking about Negroes is dominated by the impressions that cling to our brain cells after a hurried drive through the local Harlem or after a shocked glance at the photographs published so frequently of Negro problem areas.

In many cases these pictures are run to arouse our sympathy and to shock us into action. But continued emphasis on the worst Negro living conditions also strengthens fear of being engulfed in this black flood of misery.

Actually every large city has Negro residential areas that are as different as night is to day, as black is to white. In some of the worst sections of Brooklyn's Bedford-Stuyvesant slum all the indices of social trouble are double and triple the city average.

But there are neighborhoods in Queens in which Negroes predominate, where all these indices run below the city level.

Unconsciously we tend to regard the worst of the Negro areas as the "norm." We forget that many Negro slums are gateway districts into which immigrants from the South first come; that many have heavy concentrations of single men and women, with nocturnal, unfamilylike proclivities.

Certainly newspaper and TV cameras should not be shut to the misery; but they should also be open to report what Negro families have been able to do for themselves, that they have been able to shed the traits and stereotypes from which so many white people shrink.

Those Negroes who do move into middle-class neighborhoods tend to lean toward more rather than less respectability. In Chicago some middle-class Negro areas have voted themselves dry, barred store-front churches, and have even prohibited a carnival because "it was unbecoming in the neighborhood."

As Negroes become more widely dispersed through our urban communities, it should become easier for all of us to differentiate between various classes of Negroes and between individual Negroes.

Mixed streets are needed as well, so whites and Negroes can learn to live with one another. Abstract principles of social justice and equality are fine but they must walk out of the books and laws onto the streets. Earlier minority groups could move into a new neighborhood, merge quietly into the one-complexioned background and gain acceptance in time. With Negroes acceptance has to be a conscious act. Unless streets remain mixed, the consciousness of color cannot be overcome.

Still another reason why residential mobility is so vital is that it is necessary to make self-segregation possible. The term "self-segregation" may jar one's eardrums but here again the experience of previous minority groups is constructive. Each of these minority groups began their saga of Americanization by living in ethnic ghettos, where they often saw only people of their own ethnic background.

As they climbed into newer neighborhoods the degree of this concentration thinned, but generally people resegregated themselves to live with friends and relatives, with other families of the same religion or of similar educational and economic standing.

Consider, for example, two Long Island communities — Great Neck and Manhasset — not too far apart in geographical mileage or in income standing. Great Neck is almost solidly Jewish; Manhasset heavily Catholic.

Most of the husbands and wives now living in each of these communities spent their childhood on the Lower East Side of Manhattan. They resented the East Side as a ghetto, in which people were less individuals than "micks" or "kikes" or "wops."

Today, though, neither Great Neck nor Manhasset is stigmatized as a "segregated" area, although this is what they are. The crucial difference, of course, is that these families are living there by their own choice. They find it more pleasant and

comfortable than if they lived in a community with a totally
different religious background or where the stores did not
feature the foods and other delicacies that tickled their pal-
ates or where their friends and families would feel like
strangers.

There is no reason to believe that Negroes would behave
any differently. Given the choice of where to live, most of
them can be expected to prefer predominantly Negro areas
where they will feel psychologically comfortable.

But for voluntary segregation to be possible families must
first be able to detach themselves from the surroundings they
do not like and be able to regroup themselves on a basis of
self-respect and dignity.

Note the parallel between strict residential segregation in
the North and Southern insistence on preserving "colored"
and "white" taboos. As long as the taboos remain they are a
continuous reminder of personal indignity, which sharpens
resentment. Yet if they were lifted, the changes in living
would be comparatively small and, even as they spread, more
readily adjusted to.

Similarly, as long as Negroes feel imprisoned in their ghettos, the fact that they must live together inflames every irrita-
tion into a major grievance.

The longer we neglect establishing the conditions for residential mobility, the more we lose the ability to cope with the
racial problem. Lifting the barriers of residential segregation
today, for example, has been made infinitely more difficult by
the fact that so much of the Negro population has been
damned back for so long in their black belts, and by the continued influx of newcomers from the South.

There have been a few successful experiments in controlled interracial housing, such as the Quaker developments near Philadelphia, where the number of Negro families in the project is strictly limited. But, as Professor Morton Grodzins has pointed out, much more interracial experimentation is needed.

Still no amount of experimentation is likely to be adequate unless white people change their thinking about living next door to Negroes. White families must shed their psychological resistances; the Negroes must shed those traits that frighten people from living next to them.

Nor has enough been done to spread Negro residences into the suburbs. Even if these communities turn out in the end to be all-Negro, they still would serve the highly useful purpose of enabling better-income Negroes to detach themselves from the worst slums.

Suburban Negro communities might also help correct the present uneven balance between swollen Negro populations inside the cities and tiny Negro numbers in the suburbs.

This disparity in Negro numbers inside and outside the cities points to what is probably the most serious political and social cleavage in the nation. At stake is the future of all our cities. This cleavage is also likely to structure much of the political history our children will live with.

During the 1910's and 1920's the prevailing pattern of living in most urban areas was largely one of segregation, but it was segregation by economic class, with lower-income working-class neighborhoods walled off socially and economically from the silk stocking districts. Eventually these class

distinctions came to be blurred over but not until after two
generations of political conflict.

We have not even begun to narrow the Great Racial Separation. It still seems to be widening.

Often while studying maps which show how the Negro
ghettos in city after city have pushed out in an ever-widening
radius, I have thought how much like tree trunks were these
maps. The rings in the tree trunk tell us how old the tree is;
the racial rings how old the ghetto is. Each racial ring represents time that has been lost; time that is still to be paid for;
time that is the wall separating us into two nations.

Desegregation: Symbol or Reality

In both North and South one further change in racial
thinking will be needed — a more balanced look at the symbol known as segregation.

A totally unrealistic, nightmarish concept has been built up
by both Negroes and whites about what can be accomplished
through desegregation. White parents have talked about
school desegregation as if they expected it to lead to revolutionary social upheavals; to Negroes desegregation has become almost an end-all, cure-all symbol.

Both the fears of the whites and the hopes of the Negroes
have been blown up out of proportion.

Almost anyone who attended school with Negro children
in his youth can testify to the fact that mixing white and Negro children has only a marginal impact. Far from leading to
intermarriage, relatively few lasting friendships are formed

between white and colored children as the result of going to school together.

Perhaps the main benefit of school integration is that it helps shape an after-school society that is healthier for both whites and Negroes. Children in mixed schools learn more readily to think of themselves and others as human beings; they learn to prize those values which enable us to recognize achievement in any individual whatever his origin. Nor should institutions be maintained which insult the personal dignity of any part of the nation.

Negroes, for their part, have acquired a justifiable hatred of segregation itself, to a point even of blaming it for all the ills and discriminations that burden Negro living. Yet with each year that passes it will become more important for Negroes to be able to distinguish between those problems which are produced by segregation and those which would remain even if Jericho's walls came tumbling down.

Psychologically, perhaps a parallel can be drawn with colonialism. Africans and Asiatics came to look on colonial rule as the root cause of everything wrong and lacking. "Independence now" became to them the cure for every trouble.

But the burdens of India have not been lifted because the British are gone, nor is the Congo a dreamier world than when the Belgians were there. One can understand why the Indians and Africans demanded self-rule and independence but "freedom" by itself thrusts only so far.

We can also understand James Baldwin's passionate desire to batter down the walls of segregation regardless of what may lie behind the walls. Still, desegregation in itself cannot be made the single, all-encompassing goal of racial progress.

Along with efforts to break down the walls of segregation, we must find ways of improving Negro living inside these ghettos.

This must be done because there simply is no way of emptying Harlem instantly or quickly. A considerable degree of de facto segregation is certain to persist for years to come. In most Southern cities, for example, the construction of new homes has been arranged so that new housing for Negroes expands in one direction while new housing for whites pushes out in the opposite direction.

By the time Negro and white children are mixed to any great extent in the South a new pattern of school segregation through residential layout will be in existence.

In some Southern cities, in fact, resistance to quick desegregation has aimed at gaining enough time for white families to move out into Negro-free suburbs. When the Civil Rights Commission held hearings in Memphis, a savings and loan association executive testified, "Ten years ago my neighborhood was fairly mixed. Now our integrated neighborhoods are becoming completely segregated." He predicted that soon there would be no whites living anywhere within proximity of Negroes.

Similarly, New Orleans has never had a solid black residential belt as in Northern cities. The prevailing custom was for Negro and white families to live scattered through much of the city, often on the same street or only a block or two apart. In New Orleans, as in Memphis, white families are regrouping themselves into a more segregated pattern.

In the South of the future Negroes may find it more important to lift the level and quality of schooling provided in predominantly Negro schools than to enforce a token of integration.

Which constitutes the more important advance in Houston, Texas — that a few more Negroes be admitted into the elementary schools or that all Negro vocational schools be strengthened to where they teach the same trades as do the white schools?

As it is, the emphasis given desegregation may have diverted energy from the more critical need of reorganizing the curriculums of Negro schools, particularly those in the rural South. While in Selma, I was told of one Negro who was to be promoted to the job of driving a truck but couldn't get a license because he was unable to sign his name. And yet he had managed to get through the seventh grade in school.

In England, Arkansas, south of Little Rock, a local school board member related with pride how new teaching machines had been bought for the white high school so the students would be able to get the instruction in foreign languages and mathematics that was needed to qualify for college. Negroes, though, were still being taught courses in vocational agriculture — subsidized in part by the federal government — even though the nearby plantations had cut their labor needs to a tenth of what they had been a decade ago.

Many of these Negroes will eventually move North, where they will find their agricultural training about as useful in getting a job as whistling.

Of course, both inequities — of segregation and poor education — should be corrected. But to do so may require separate actions.

In principle the obvious solution is to permit Negroes and white children to attend the same schools, and this battle should be pressed with the fullest possible zeal. But for some years to come, Negroes will still be schooled separately; they should not be taught vocations that are obsolete.

Both actions need to be pressed to reduce the burden of adjustment. The schools in the South will continue to turn out students, many of whom will come North, who are poorly trained.

The first goal should be better education in all schools. We need to reach in and get at all these schools.

Another pressing need is to determine the *causes* for the poor schooling that seems so prevalent in many predominantly Negro schools. In the South, inferior Negro education has been tied to segregation. Negro children have been forced to attend all-Negro schools with inadequately trained teachers, dilapidated buildings, and low school standards. Less money was spent on Negro schools.

Many Northern school systems, though, do not spend less on predominantly Negro schools than on all-white schools. Still, all-Negro schools in these cities suffer from serious deficiencies.

The segregationist-minded would attribute this poor educational performance to an innate mental inferiority of the Negroes. Many Negro leaders, for their part, appear determined to pin the fault upon the fact that Negroes live under segregated, "culturally deprived" conditions. One outstanding Negro psychologist, Dr. Kenneth Clark, argues eloquently that the basic trouble is poor teaching, that teachers in Negro schools have abandoned all efforts to really teach Negro children.

Here as well one suspects that no overall generalization covers the whole problem. Certainly individual Negro children are born with varying capacities, even as are white children. More inspired teaching would help somewhat. Also a large part of the problem probably reflects economic and cultural difficulties which are beyond the reach of the schools.

Since no doctor can say with finality what sickness is "incurable," we should continue experimenting with new ways of meeting these problems. At the same time though, we should press for a cause and effect analysis of why some Negro students do well and others do not, of how much can be accomplished by changes inside the schools and how much hinges on changes in the rest of society. How much of the difficulty stems from community disorganization? From family back-ground? From low motivation? From the limitations of the individual?

Such a determination would be a vital aid in guiding racial bargaining into more constructive channels. In some cities, like New York, the transfer of Negro children into predominantly white schools has gone on long enough so that the factual evidence should be available to determine what these transfers accomplish and what they do not do.

Unfortunately the New York City school board sits on this evidence, lacking the courage and wit to make it public.

What constitutes real integration?

A painter's wife in Brooklyn recalled, "I was terribly upset when I learned my daughter was being sent to a high school in a depressed area. But it hasn't done her any harm. She's in the general acceleration course. There aren't any Negroes in her class.

"It isn't really integration," she went on. "The students inside the school are divided into brighter classes, less bright and so on. Segregation exists in these classes with the top ones being all white and the low ones being practically all Negro."

The wife of a business executive contended, "It really isn't desegregation because after school the Negro children go back to their own neighborhood. They can't participate in after-school activities because they don't live in the neighborhood and have to take a bus home right after school."

Across the whole broad front of Negro demands we need factual determinations of what will help lift the handicaps that Negroes labor under and what actions are likely to prove meaningless gestures, needless disruptions for the rest of society. Standards of effective integration are indispensable for sound racial adjustment, for laying out goals that both races can work toward, for balancing white fears and Negro hopes.

Through the whole of Negro living there is also a desperate need for more energetic efforts by Negroes themselves to correct many of the ills that plague them. Negroes differ in their problems from old-time immigrant groups. Still, after allowance is made for these differences, as is brought out so well by Nathan Glazer in *Beyond the Melting Pot*, there is no question but that Negroes and their leaders have not done as much as they could to help themselves.

The Negro's problems are aggravated enormously by his being treated as an inferior, and it is the responsibility of white society to accord the Negro the dignity and respect that he can rise to. But there are enough examples of what individual Negroes have been able to do on their own to make clear that many more Negroes can do more with themselves.

Finally, we must admit to ourselves that many Negro aspirations clash strongly with other American values and with some of the trends of change that dominate American life today.

How does one deliver on the promise of "freedom now," for example, in a society which is not literally free for any American? Wherever one looks in this country there are at least as many fences as open fields. The seniority that ensures the job to the older worker walls out the newer, younger worker; the hedgerow or shrubs that give one family privacy shuts neighbors out of sight. Urban living necessarily has to be segregated living to some degree.

This is not to argue that the cause of individual civil liberty is a hopeless one. We know much more can be done to reduce and eliminate discrimination. However, full "freedom" is beyond the reach of any of us. When it comes to implementing specific "rights" we are likely to find that they clash with other worthy objectives and valued institutions.

Some trends of American living add their complications. A strong family structure, for example, is indispensable for climbing out of a slum. Yet the newer fashions in living, such as looser sexual morals and divorce, tend to weaken the family structure.

Also much of the basis of the immigrant ideal is being undermined. The immigrant climb was made possible by parents who restricted their own spending and consumption in order to provide their children with advantages that had been denied themselves. Today, though, the emphasis on saving is enfeebled by such practices as installment buying and by doctrines that extol spending as the newest economic virtue.

With Negroes the family structure is particularly important. Slavery often separated fathers from their wives and children, which left a weak family structure. Although this weakness is being lessened, it still persists because many Negro women find it easier to obtain employment than do Negro men.*

*The need to halt "the breakdown of the Negro family" was given dramatic publicity in the summer of 1965 in the Moynihan Report. The statistics cited in this report were bone-chilling indeed — that one Negro family in four is fatherless; more than a third of all Negro Children live in broken homes; that nearly a fourth of all Negro babies are born out of wedlock.

But the Moynihan Report, admittedly, contains no diagnosis that can serve as a basis for directed action. The report puts the brunt of blame for weak Negro families on slavery which, it is argued, "emasculated the Negro male."

While the heritage of slavery is important, the fact that most Negroes, when given a decent economic chance, do rear stable families, suggests that more recent happenings are to blame.

Much of the current demoralization of low-income Negro families has arisen out of the socially disruptive migration of so many Negroes from the rural South into Northern cities.

The ill effects of rural uprooting need to be minimized at both ends of Migration Road.

In the South the necessary action is to halt the buildup of neglects, such as scanty education, which rural Negroes bring with them when they move to the city.

A second disturbing trend of change in American living is the new emphasis on group interests that appears to be gaining ascendency in our society. Years ago when people were asked what was the biggest difference between the parties, the reply usually ran, "The Republicans bring hard times; the Democrats bring prosperity."

During recent years references to the depression have dropped out of people's talk. More and more the differences between Democrats and Republicans are seen in terms of the economic groups each party is supposed to favor.

In some ways this is strange. Certainly differences between the rich and the poor have narrowed. There is also less of a gulf between farm and urban living, between one section of the country and another. One would expect conflict between groups and classes to be easing rather than growing more intense.

This intensifying group conflict, I believe, reflects the expanded part that government is playing in our lives. The way in which taxes and subsidies fall touches off a struggle of group interests. The individual as an individual has been losing importance. More and more he is forced to take his place in the economic lineup as a member of a union, trade association, an age group, or a racial group.

The widening use of computers add to the pressures to lose sight of the individual and to lump him into some statistical grouping.

In the North action needs to be directed at the special problems of these immigrants, such as, their difficulties in finding work and in becoming part of a strange new community which imposes so much less social discipline than prevails in the rural South.

A stable family, in short, is the end product of a host of influences.

In short, a managed economy seems to breed and to necessitate group consciousness and even group conflict. Defining group relations, in turn, tends to become an exercise in group bargaining. Each group soon learns that it can enforce its demands best by threatening a crisis to which the governing powers can yield so as to preserve peace.

If this observation is valid, then many current trends of change must be operating to keep alive group differences in racial as well as economic terms, to deprive us of our ability to see Negroes as individuals and to force us to deal with them as members of a distinctive race.

Here we have a real conflict.

Certainly many governmental benefits that have been handed out — from aid to dependent children, welfare rolls, public housing subsidies, urban renewal — have tended to perpetuate the pattern of residential segregation and racial differentiation in our cities.

Negro leaders, as well, have been trying to condition their people to think of voting as members of a united bloc rather than as individuals.

Some white "liberals," like Daniel P. Moynihan, have begun to argue for "group equality." In his report on the Negro family, Moynihan contends, "it is increasingly demanded that the distribution of success and failure within one group be roughly comparable to that within other groups."

Right now, Negroes must utilize group action to the fullest advantage. But to elevate "group equality" into a political creed would institutionalize racial conflict, much as Karl Marx sought to institutionalize "class war" of economic groups. Even if each person's living standard was to leap upward, differences between individuals, and therefore "groups," would persist.

If American society fails to treat Negroes as individuals, then they will remain a separate group — more accurately a subnation — in our midst. I believe we should make the fight for equality of opportunity for the individual before accepting group conflict as a political ideal or political norm.

To repeat, during the immediate years ahead we will have little choice but to continue to deal with Negroes, as they are — a separate, segregated subnation. But we should look beyond the next few elections and seek to root out the conditions that would make Negroes a permanent minority, as with the French-speaking people of Quebec or the distinct nationality enclaves that persist in European countries.

Time is an investment that both pays and charges interest. We can spend it strengthening or weakening any characteristic of society; we can spend it on those characteristics which will intensify the Negro's sense of racialism or on those which lighten it.

Currently Negro militants act and talk as if theirs were the "absolute" cause to which all other considerations must bow. Yet there are contradictions within the demands being pressed by the Negroes. These demands will have to be harmonized with other American values.

With time, as well, prevailing trends of American life will

change. We cannot anticipate these changes now. For the immediate years ahead what should be done is to give the Negro his proper place in the arena of American democracy.

This does not mean that the Negro should be conceded everything he demands. Constructive resistance is needed to get him to understand the contradictions in his own values. But it does mean that we should let him come into the arena on the same basis as anyone else, with the same chance to fight to advance himself, even as we, the rest of the people, battle to advance ourselves.

Reading Notes

Simply to catalogue the wealth of writings on Negro affairs would require a book in itself. The most that can be attempted in these pages is to note some of the books and articles that proved most helpful. Still the reader should be warned that no effort was made to read everything that has been written and many volumes of worth have undoubtedly not been included.

Gunnar Myrdal's *An American Dilemma* (1944) remains the best single over-all reference work for the period up to the end of World War II.

Not well known but quite rewarding is Richard Bardolph's *Negro Vanguard* (1959), a highly readable study of Negro leadership since Emancipation.

For a good general textual survey of Negro history see John Hope Franklin's *From Slavery to Freedom,* revised and enlarged edition, 1956.

Chapter 1.   Racial Showdown

The new mood of militancy that characterizes the Negro today can be grasped best, of course, from the day's headlines. The

writings of James Baldwin are particularly eloquent; Louis
Lomax's *The Negro Revolt* (1962) yields some sense of the
desire of the newer militants to challenge the older Negro leadership. See also *The New Negro* edited by Matthew H. Ahmann
(1961).

The Southern Education Reporting Service is the source for
the calculation that in the eleven southern states only 12,868
Negro children (.453% of the total) were attending schools
with white children at the end of the 1962–63 school year.

Chapter 2.   The Great Tranquilizer

The controversial place of Booker T. Washington in Negro history is ably discussed in the symposium entitled *Booker T.
Washington and His Critics,* edited by Hugh Hawkins of Am-
herst College (1962).

Washington's own writings reveal much about the man, particularly if read in the sequence in which his books were published, bearing in mind the steady loss of Negro rights even as
each successive volume was written.

His books were:

1899–*Future of the American Negro*
1900–*Sowing and Reaping*
1901–*Up From Slavery*
1904–*Working with the Hands*
1906–*Putting Most into Life*
1907–*Life of Frederick Douglass*
1909–*Story of the Negro*
1911–*My Larger Education*
1912–*The Man Farthest Down*

Two comparatively recent biographies of Washington have
been written by Basil Mathews (1948) and Samuel Spencer
(issued in 1955).

For a revealing account of the status of the Southern Negro

in Booker T. Washington's day, see the article in the *Journal of Negro History* (1958) by Clarence Bacote on "Some Aspects of Negro Life in Georgia 1880–1908."

Rayford Logan's *The Negro in American Life and Thought: The Nadir, 1877–1901* (1954) is a good general survey of the Washington era.

The quote about the Negro being given equal consideration with the mule came from William Watts Ball, *The Editor and the Republic*.

Vann Woodward's *Origins of the New South* (1951) has become the classic for this period, while his *The Strange Career of Jim Crow* (1954) supplies the best brief cataloguing of the origins of segregation. Thomas J. Woofter, Jr.'s, *Negro Migration* chronicles the rise of the sharecropper as a lowly institution and the slow death of the large plantations.

Chapter 3. *Black Nationalism*

Despite its drama and importance, no really definitive account exists of the northward migration of the Negro during the World War I period. Much of what has been written has been drawn from the report on "The Negro in Chicago" of the Chicago Commission on Race Relations in 1921–22.

Negro Migration During the War (1920), by Emmett J. Scott, is another primary source. Louise Kennedy's *The Negro Peasant Turns Cityward* (1930) presents a fine picture of the conditions which greeted the Southern blacks in most Northern cities.

A good summation of how the South tried to prevent the Negro's emigration during World War I is contained in an article by Leo Alilunas in *Journal of Negro History* (1937).

Francis L. Broderick has written the most complete biography of W. E. B. Du Bois; Elliot M. Rudwick also deals with his career in a more specialized form, *W.E.B. Du Bois: A Study in Minority Group Leadership* (1960).

Of Du Bois's own prolific writings, I found his earliest works most revealing. In *The Souls of Black Folk* (1903) Du Bois was the first writer to show how partial freedom tended to make the Negro a split personality. His sociological study on Negroes in Philadelphia toward the end of the century is intriguing in that some of his observations on the reactions of whites to Negroes could be repeated today.

In *The Lonely Warrior* (1955) Roi Ottley gives both a vivid portrait of Robert Abbott and some discussion of the role of the Negro press in strengthening Negro racial consciousness.

David E. Cronon's *Black Moses* (1955) is a lively, revealing biography of Marcus Garvey.

Eric Lincoln's *Black Muslims in America* (1961) is the best available survey of this movement.

Chapter 4.   The Roosevelt Revolution

More has been written about Negro politics in Chicago than in any other American city. The best accounts will be found in *Black Metropolis* by H. R. Cayton and St. Clair Drake (1945); Harold Gosnell's *Negro Politicians* (1935) and John Q. Wilson's stimulating *Negro Politics*.

The political antics of Mayor Thompson are recounted in *Big Bill of Chicago* by Lloyd Wendt and Herman Kogan (1953).

In New York the number of political clubs and their party affiliation in the 1930's comes from *The Political Clubs of New York City* (1935) by Roy V. Peel. Fernando Wood's flirtation with the idea of New York seceding from the Union is recounted in M. R. Werner's *Tammany Hall* (1928).

Later Negro political developments are treated well in both *Harlem: Negro Metropolis* (1940) by Claude McKay, and Roi Ottley's *New World A Comin'* (1955).

The formation of the Roosevelt coalition and its revolutionary impact upon Negroes is dealt with in my *The Future of American Politics* (1952). Arthur Schlesinger's *The Coming of the New Deal* (1959) gives a good account of the spread of race relations advisers through the New Deal agencies.

For the effects of the depression on Negroes and other workers see *The Lean Years* by Irving Bernstein (1960).

For the impact of the CIO, see *Black Workers and the New Unions* (1939) by George S. Mitchell and H. R. Cayton. In his autobiography, *A Man Called White* (1948), Walter White tells how Negro auto workers at Ford were finally organized by the CIO. A fuller account of the Ford strike is contained in *Ford: Decline and Rebirth* (1962) by Allan Nevins and Frank Ernest Hill.

H. R. Northrup's *Organized Labor and the Negro* (1944) is a good chronicle of developments until 1944. The speeches and magazine articles of Herbert Hill of the NAACP provide the best picture of racial prejudice that still prevails in unions.

The Negro's role as a strikebreaker is treated quite well in *Black Worker* by Sterling D. Spero and Abram L. Harris (1931). For a vivid glimpse into how deep-rooted was the antagonism of white and Negro workers see the *Autobiography of Frederick Douglass* (page 239) and his account of the troubles he experienced while working in a Baltimore shipyard.

The Changed Political Thought of the Negro, 1915–40 (1951) by Elbert Lee Tatum is particularly good in assessing the revolutionary new political role that became possible for the Negro with his exodus from the South.

Henry L. Moon's *Balance of Power* (1948) provides a compact summary of Negro political history up to 1948, although I do not accept his thesis that Negroes hold the balance of power in presidential elections. John G. Van Deusen's *Black Man in White America* (1944) is stimulating in its interpretative judgments.

In the fall 1963 issue of the *Journal of Negro Education*

Harold F. Gosnell and Robert E. Martin estimate that 3,000,000 Negroes outside of the South voted in 1960. (This assumes that 60% of adult Negroes vote.) Such a vote would yield the Democrats a plurality of more than a million.

Chapter 5.   Battle for the South

The importance attached to the projection of the Negro-labor alliance into the South is emphasized in the writings of Walter White (see *How Far the Promised Land,* 1955); also Moon's *Balance of Power.*

Why the white South turned more conservative politically in the 1950's is explained in my *The Future of American Politics* and *Revolt of the Moderates* (1956). For a discussion of Southern attitudes to economic expansion see William H. Nichols' *Southern Tradition and Regional Progress.*

Much of the biographical material about the family of Martin Luther King, Jr., is drawn from L. D. Reddick's *Crusader Without Violence* (1959) and King's own *Stride Toward Freedom* (1958).

Margaret Price's *The Negro Vote in the South* and *The Negro and the Ballot* are revealing accounts of the efforts to increase Negro suffrage. Both are Southern Regional Council Pamphlets.

Chapter 6.   The Second Civil War

Most of the material on how white Southerners and Negroes reacted to the school desegregation decision is drawn from my own interviews in the South during these years. My feeling that an armed clash was impending between the federal and state governments was expressed in an article in *Commentary,* April 1957.

John Bartlow Martin's *Deep South Says Never* (1957) catches the mood of resistance that characterizes the White Citizens Council. The Southern Regional Council's *Intimidation, Reprisal and Violence in the South's Racial Crisis* is another depressing but revealing chronicle.

For what was happening in the White House during the earlier years of Southern resistance see Sherman Adams's *Firsthand Report* (1961), Emmet John Hughes's *The Ordeal of Power* (1963), and *Black Man in the White House* by E. Frederic Morrow (1963). But none of these accounts seems really to explain Eisenhower's "inside" thinking.

We can only hope for more frankness in the soon-to-appear memoirs of the insiders in the Kennedy Administration on how and why President Kennedy equivocated with the civil rights issue during the first years of his Administration.

An Epitaph for Dixie by Harry S. Ashmore (1957) reveals the frustrations felt by liberal Southerners before the turning point in the integration war.

The Reports of the U.S. Commission on Civil Rights often provide excellent accounts of the racial conflict in specific states or cities.

Chapter 7.   The Crisis Moves North

Charles E. Silberman's *The City and the Negro* in *Fortune,* March 1962, is a good account of what the Negro's northward migration has done to our cities.

The percentages cited of the proportion of Negroes in the public schools came from the Boards of Education in those cities.

A compact summary of Negro economic progress will be found in Emmet J. Hughes's article in *Fortune,* September 1956.

The Journal of Negro Education's issues in the summer of 1953 and the fall of 1963 provide a comparative evaluation of the standing of the Negro in the two periods.

Chapter 8.   The Politics of Race

E. Franklin Frazier's *Black Bourgeoisie* (1957) is an excellent study of the Negro middle class.

The listing of America's most influential Negroes will be found in *Ebony,* September, 1963, Emancipation issue.

The rise in the Republican vote in the South has followed this pattern:

1932	18%
1936	19%
1940	18.9%
1944	25%
1948	27%
1952	37%
1956	49%
1960	46%

The resistance of Democratic voters to local measures that would require tax increases has been documented by Prof. Marko Haggard of Portland (Oregon) State College; see also *The Rulers and the Ruled* by Robert E. Agger, Daniel Goodrich and Bert E. Swanson.

Chapter 9.   Toward Racial Peace

An excellent picture of the effects of the Negro concentration in the major cities will be found in the reports of Prof. Morton Grodzins of the University of Chicago.

For a particularly sensitive and revealing account of how Negroes differ from other minority groups see *Beyond the Melting Pot* by Nathan Glazer and Daniel Moynihan (1963).

Index

ABOUT THE AUTHOR

In *Who's Who,* Samuel Lubell gives his occupation as "writer" —a term that covers a remarkably versatile talent. He has been a newspaperman, foreign correspondent, and magazine writer; he has also been a White House aide, and he served as principal assistant to Bernard M. Baruch on all his famous World War II and postwar studies.

For his writing on politics, Mr. Lubell has developed a unique "time machine" approach which allows him to see politics as a ceaseless struggle between the past and the future and the electorate as the arena in which the struggle is taking place. He probes, by means of interviews, for the meaning of elections and the trends of change remaking American society. These reporter-historian techniques have enabled Mr. Lubell to predict with surprising accuracy the outcome of every presidential and off-year election since 1952. On repeated election nights he has announced the winner before the computers by projecting the vote of a small number of precincts.

Mr. Lubell is the author of three other books: *The Future of American Politics, Revolt of the Moderates* and *Revolution in World Trade.* His election reports and columns on public opinion appear regularly in more than a hundred newspapers. He is also Director of the Opinion Reporting Workshop at Columbia University's Graduate School of Journalism.

COLOPHON BOOKS ON POLITICAL SCIENCE

*In Preparation